God's Spirit

Transforming
a World in Crisis

Geiko Müller-Fahrenholz

. . . .

God's Spirit

Transforming
a World in Crisis

CONTINUUM · NEW YORK

WCC PUBLICATIONS · GENEVA

1995

The Continuum Publishing Company
370 Lexington Avenue
New York, NY 10017

World Council of Churches
Conseil Oecumenique des Eglises
150 route de Ferney
1211 Geneva 2, Switzerland

Translated by John Cumming from the *German Erwecke die Welt:*
Unser Glaube an Gottes Geist in dieser bedrohten Zeit published by
Gütersloher Verlagshaus/Kaiser, Gütersloh, 1993.
This translation (c) World Council of Churches, Geneva, 1995.

Library of Congress Cataloging-in-Publication Data

Müller-Fahrenholz, Geiko.
God's spirit: transforming a world in crisis / Geiko Müller-Fahrenholz.
p. cm.
Includes bibliographical references.
ISBN 0-8264-0824-9 (alk. paper)
1. Holy Spirit. 2. Spiritual life. 3. Human ecology–Religious aspects–
Christianity. 4. Church and the world. I. Title
BT 121. 2.M854 1995
231' .3–dc20   95-12831
                                                  CIP

WCC ISBN: 2-8254-1158-2

Printed in the United States of America

For Tina-Marei and Manuel

Contents

Foreword

I am pleased to have the opportunity to write the foreword to the English edition of this book, *God's Spirit: Transforming a World in Crisis*, by my friend Geiko Müller-Fahrenholz. After reading the German version for the first time, I wrote that "this book is a godsend. It is the best thing I have read in recent years. The author combines bold new ideas with his own experiences in the ecumenical movement, in Germany and in the third world" (where he then lived). Rereading the book before writing this foreword confirmed my initial impression: again I discovered new and startling insights as well as remarkable formulations.

The author begins almost every section with questions and ideas that are familiar to professional theologians, but time and again his train of thought takes an unexpected turn, affording the reader new and surprising perspectives that prompt original thoughts. Our imaginations are stirred regarding the kingdom of God in the world, and we find ourselves discovering the action of the Spirit of God in history. That is the result of the novel way of thinking in this book, which is as theologically profound as it is practically relevant. If this "applied pneumatology" were to become the new "practical ecumenical theology", we would no longer need to be worried about ecumenical theology.

Something emerges here from the content and style which is obviously not possible in the traditions of confessional theology. The author strives towards "ecumenical pastoral care", in other words, a practical congregational theology whose framework and key ideas should be applicable everywhere. That is rather ambitious and could easily give rise to erroneous conjecture, since a person who tries to say something to everyone will ultimately says nothing useful to anyone. The very lesson we have learned from the movements of "contextual theology", liberation theology, black theology, *minjung* theology and feminist theology, is that theology must be specific, not general, and that it cannot be objective and without subject. All theological reflection belongs in its own kairos, in its own place and to its particular subjects.

Geiko Müller-Fahrenholz is well aware of this; yet in this book he discloses common global situations that correspond to common attitudes of the human soul. The ecological crisis — which, following the United Nations conferences in Rio de Janeiro in 1992 and Berlin in 1995, may be described as the onset of a global environmental disaster — is occurring not only externally in such realities as the destruction of the ozone layer and increasing desertification, but also internally in the psychic numbing of the earth's human inhabitants. A central thesis of this book is that there is a profound interaction between external violence and inner violence. Drawing on the idea of "numbing" developed by the US psychologist Robert J. Lifton, the author amply elucidates this in the second part of this book, "Creator Spirit — Soul of My Soul". His excellent chapters on contemporary cynicism, fundamentalism and violentism help us to a better grasp of our own situation.

For the author, however, what is at stake here is not just a new reading of the signs of the times, but practical theology. By construing this numbing as *acedia, tristesse* — correctly, I think — he is already addressing the essence of the doctrine of sin, which leads to death. In his practical theology, Geiko Müller-Fahrenholz invites us to rethink basic theological concepts in the light of today's global experiences of life and death. In a surprising way, he brings to light theological ideas which have not so far been in the forefront of ecumenical theology and ethics: the doctrines of sin, forgiveness, reconciliation and consolation. He interprets these both personally and politically, helping to bridge the age-old gulf between "ecumenical" and "evangelical". He shows in Chapter 15 how the biblical idea of "consolation" must be freed from the connotations which it has acquired of piously "cheering people up" or "calming them down". Chapter 20, "The Reality of Solidarity in the Ecodomical Covenant", is particularly well-written.

And I could go on and on, continuing as it were to throw light on new facets of a gem. But I shall leave that to the reader, whom I invite to embark on a journey of discovery.

Tübingen   *Jürgen Moltmann*
April 1995

Introduction

Two observations have led me to write this book.

First, as we approach the end of the second millennium after Christ, humanity has become the subject of its own possible self-destruction. While the nuclear threat is far from over, the impoverishment of thousands of millions of human beings and the reckless warfare against nature are now seen to be equally dangerous. Each of these factors is in itself a major challenge; their mutual connectedness turns them into a syndrome of problems that is unprecedented. Thus people have begun to talk more and more about the "ungovernability" of the world. They have growing distrust for large political bureaucracies and many are opting for violent "solutions".

Second, the increasing complexities and risks of our epoch are mirrored in our psychic disposition. The "outward" threats correspond with "inward" fatigue and restlessness. The greater the challenges become, the more difficult it is to deny them. The chaotic and ecocidal trends of today are beginning to exhaust the "carrying capacities" of our souls; hence we go numb. This numbing accounts for the tendency of people to withdraw from complicated political scenarios and for the massive epidemic of fundamentalisms around the globe.

In this context, Christian theology today dare not hide itself in the comfortable niches of confessional questions or academic disputes. It must come to terms with the fact that it too is part of the global connectedness and therefore part of the problem. Theology that tries to be relevant to our critical conditions is by nature ecumenical. It relies on the voices of women and men from around the world and from all religions; in particular, it draws on the wisdom of those who suffer most from today's trials.

Therefore, it is not enough for Christian theology to address political, economic or social issues in purely propositional and theoretical terms. It also needs to respond to the emotional anguish; it must speak to the pain and despair that make our hearts sick and kill our imagination. It is my firm conviction that theological thinking should make a conscious effort to combine systematic analysis with pastoral awareness. It must acknowledge the mutuality of the "outer" and the "inner", the reciprocity of the scientific and the personal, the political and the psychological realms of life, a reciprocity which defies our customary distinction between "pure" and "applied" science and the social hierarchies which correspond to it.

It seemed obvious, therefore, to concentrate on God's Spirit, that dimension of the Trinity which has been notoriously overlooked by classical "God-talk", exactly because it is the reality "in between" the Father and the Son, "in between" the Creator and the cosmos. As I studied the biblical accounts, it soon became apparent that the Spirit is much more than the heart and soul of Pentecostal awakenings and sanctified living. It is the core-energy of creation itself. The Hebrew Bible calls it the *rûah*, the female-motherly power alive in wild storms and gentle breezes, the breath of life and therefore — incarnated in Jesus — the true image of creative, unremitting love. So as we begin to grasp this dimension of God as the power-in-between-all-things, we are able to connect the cosmic and the personal and the social. That explains why this book has three parts. The first speaks of the "Soul of the World", that is the Spirit as cosmic power. The second part goes on to discuss the "Soul of My Soul", that is the Creator Spirit as psychic power. The third then proceeds to deal with the "Soul of Christian Communities", thereby addressing the *pneuma* as social and ecclesial power.

"God is Spirit," says the gospel of John (4:24). That is the perspective set forth in this book. It connects creation theology with pastoral care and ecclesiology because it is one and the same transformative power which sustains the unfolding of the universe, endows each being with a sense of self and provides communities with purpose and dedication.

It might be illuminating to add a biographical note. In the 1970s I was privileged to work in the Geneva-based central offices of the World Council of Churches. Daily encounters with colleagues from all corners of the world and constant exposure to global problems gave me a firsthand impression of the tasks that confront humankind.

For most of the 1980s I was back in my home church, the Lutheran Church in Germany, directing a centre for adult and youth education. Working with various issue-groups and grass-roots organizations led me to appreciate the local implications and psychological pressures of global needs.

From 1989 to 1993 I lived in Costa Rica, where I taught ecumenical theology and ecological ethics to students from many countries in Central and South America. They helped me to get a clearer picture of the daily sufferings which the dominant world economic disorder is causing in the so-called third world — where in fact two-thirds of the world's people live and die.[1]

I mention these three very different experiences because they will help to explain why I am indebted to a great variety of authors, notably from the areas of liberation theology, feminist theology, indigenous studies and pastoral psychology. I am especially grateful to Robert Jay Lifton; for his works have helped me enormously to understand the phenomenon of numbing. But I am also acutely aware that the sources from which I have drawn may appear to be rather eclectic; there is no doubt in my mind that I must have overlooked significant materials.

This English translation is about one-fourth shorter than the German original; several chapters have been omitted, others extensively rewritten and many bibliographical references (largely to German works) left out. The resulting brevity of argument accents the programmatic character of the book.

A special word of thanks must go to John Cumming for his translation and to Marlin VanElderen from the World Council of Churches' Office of Publications for his editorial care.

My wife and I have often agonized about the fact that we are bequeathing a vastly endangered world to those whom we love most, our children. So I am dedicating this book to our daughter, Tina-Marei, and our son, Manuel. Their rights to a life worth living and their hopes for a planet full of splendour and awe were on my mind as I wrote this book.

I shall be gratified if the readers of the following chapters will have the same experience I had while writing them. My encounters with the transforming power of God's Spirit enabled me to see the goodness and glory in all creation, in spite of all the gloom and despair. The great English mystic Julian of Norwich was right when she insisted: "We are loved from before the beginning."

Geiko Müller-Fahrenholz

NOTE

[1] While some object to the term "third world" on the ground that it seems inherently to set up an order of importance among the nations of the world, it has been adopted as a convenient shorthand by, among others, the Ecumenical Association of Third World Theologians and the Ecumenical Coalition on Third World Tourism. The term (derived from the French *tiers-monde*) was originally used to refer to the so-called "non-aligned" countries, which sought to stay out of the sphere of influence of either the capitalist ("first world") and communist ("second world") countries, a meaning which is no longer applicable in the "post-cold war" period. Among proposed substitutes, "the South" is geographically imprecise, "underdeveloped [or "developing"] countries" conveys a particular ideology of "development" and "two-thirds world" is statistically dubious and linguistically awkward. The term "third world" is also used to point to the growing "awareness gap" between people in the industrialized nations and those in the impoverished regions of the earth. Although our planet is often described as a "global village", people are in fact living in different "worlds". For the sake of convenience, the term "third world", despite its limitations and the risk that it may blur the real distinctions among and within these countries, is thus used in this book.

Part I

Creator Spirit
Soul of the World

Chapter 1

Come, Creator Spirit!

"Veni, Creator Spiritus!" These are the first three words of a well-known Pentecost hymn by Rabanus Maurus (776-856). But "Come, Creator Spirit!" is not just the first line of a hymn. It is a cry: an exclamation of longing and an appeal.

This appeal recalls the entreaty of the first Christians: *"Maranatha"*, "Our Lord, come!" (1 Cor. 16:22; cf. Rev. 22:20). Neither in Paul nor in the Apocalypse of John is this petition a mere pious refrain. It is a vital expression of all the suffering of communities living under persecution.

Over the centuries, whenever persecution or death has threatened to overwhelm believers, they have concentrated all their need and all their hope in this cry for the presence of the Lord Jesus and his *pneuma*. Amidst the afflictions of our own age, then, it was quite appropriate for the World Council of Churches to choose "Come, Holy Spirit — renew the whole creation!" as the theme of its seventh assembly (Canberra 1991). The voices heard in Canberra did reveal unmistakably the painful face of our day, even if the assembly, in the short time available to it, was unable to elicit the full implications of this prayer because of the quite diverse circumstances and convictions that delegates brought with them and the profound disorientation that the Gulf war cast over the meeting.

The meaning of this appeal is still urgently with us. "Come, Creator Spirit!" remains our petition.

It is the lament of people whose consciences are haunted by nightmarish images of millions of starving human beings and of so many children dying in torment.

It is the groan of those who cannot stomach the vicious devastation of nature.

It is the deep sigh of those who cannot tolerate being numbly accustomed to violence and injustice, and who refuse to allow the ruin of the world to paralyze their own spiritual and mental faculties.

This book emerged from the same cry. In it I do not wish to speak *about* the Spirit but to present a series of reflections arising from the prayer *for* the Spirit to come.

In Latin the first verse of Rabanus Maurus' hymn reads:

Veni, creator spiritus,
mentes tuorum visita,
imple superna gratia
quae tu creasti pectora.

In the familiar 300-year-old English version of Cosin, these lines read:

Come, Holy Ghost, our souls inspire,
And lighten with celestial fire;
Thou the anointing Spirit art,
Who dost thy sevenfold gifts impart.

Literally, the Latin means:

"*Come, Creator Spirit* (the Greek *pneuma* and the Hebrew *rûah* lie behind the Latin *spiritus*). *Visit the understanding* (actually in the plural: the mental powers) *of your people. With grace descending from above, fill the breast* (that is, the heart and lungs, feelings and disposition) *of those whom you have created.*"

On closer examination, these petitions seem oddly contradictory. The one described as Creator is to come, yet is already present. This Creator Spirit is to visit those who are already his. He is to "fill" those whom he has made, that is, to enliven the hearts and minds of people who without him were not alive at all. The series of apparently antithetical statements which the prayer develops are reminiscent of the prologue to the gospel of John: "He was in the world, and the world came into being through him; yet the world did not know him. He came to what was his own, and his own people did not accept him..." (1:10-11).

The starting-point of this ancient hymn is what Karl Barth called the "impossible possibility" that we are creations of God's Spirit and yet infinitely remote from him, that we live by his breath and yet are weary unto death. The cry for the closeness of the *pneuma* emerges from the experience of emptiness, overwhelming alienation, abandonment and confusion. The prayer evokes the loss of the Spirit's presence, the deathly torpor that grips us when God's living breath no longer suffuses head and heart, reason and emotion. Consequently, it is a prayer for something more fundamental than gifts or objects: a disclosure of the Spirit's presence, an end to confusion, an infusion of grace. In effect, it appeals to God's Spirit to show himself to be who he is.

From Rabanus Maurus we learn that to pray for God's Spirit is to seek assurance and authentic harmony. We make these petitions in the hope that beneath our entreaties an appropriate answer is already taking shape and that in our very appeal to the Spirit, the Spirit is already moving out towards us. It is not a matter of invoking a transcendent power to deliver us *from* this or that affliction or distress — that would be to instrumentalize the *pneuma* — but of experiencing the "encounter" in which all real life is rooted[1] and the sometimes only momentarily apparent presence of the Spirit *in* our need. Whenever this happens we are touched by the most precious of all things: by *superna gratia*, by *charis*, by grace as if from another world. In such moments our lamentation becomes thanksgiving and our mouth is "filled with laughter" (Ps. 126:2). Then we sing and celebrate our gratitude, culminating in the eucharist, the feast of thanksgiving.

But it sometimes happens that we have to hold on to this cry and remain within the realm of complaint, lamentation, disappointment and anger. Even then we retain a quiet hope that perhaps the breath of God is waiting to come, interceding for us "with sighs too deep for words" (Rom. 8:26).

Prayer typically consists of a series of interwoven assertions of various kinds — petition, assurance, complaint, consolation. The basic reason for this is that God's breath, God's *pneuma*, communicates itself in our own breath, so that our appeal for God's nearness already takes place in the medium of the *pneuma*. Even so, we want to understand this kind of communication better. What are we really doing when we pray?

Many people nowadays, including people within the church, feel uncomfortable about prayer. To whom are we talking when we call on Christ or the holy *rûah*? Are we just speaking to ourselves? Do we create our own interlocutor? Is our prayer only a device to help us conceal our essential alienation and emptiness?

I shall try to answer this question with a train of thought which at first may appear to be an elaborate evasion. When we pray we leave the realm of communication in which we usually operate. We depart from the sphere of rational, purposive discourse and move into that of *symbolic-mythic communication*. Such communication does not have to do with information about the objects, processes and circumstances that fill our everyday life. Instead, it seeks assurance about what ultimately maintains and concerns us. It is an encounter with the ground of all being.

This is not something restricted to religious people. All human beings have essentially mythic experiences and operate, sometimes unconsciously, in the realm of symbolic-mythic discourse. The exchange of gifts is an example of symbolic interaction. In the birth of a child or in someone's death, in the ecstasy of love or in a magnificently flowering tree, in an infinite number of major and minor moments of life, we are affected by another reality. This other reality is qualitatively distinct from the general run of things. The objectifying language of our everyday pursuits cannot properly grasp it. In such moments we sense that we are encompassed by a mystery that our words and gestures can represent only in a roundabout way. And so we use words that have layers of meaning, symbolic words and signs that help us to point to something that eludes more precise characterization.

To put it in visual terms, we scan the horizon when we look at it but know at the same time that we can never encompass it. Yet the horizon is important, for it is the circumference of our existence. Similarly, all symbolic talk and action form part of our concern to be certain of the ground underlying our speaking and behaving. Our symbols refer to the myth by which we try to describe what we look on as the ungrounded ground of our life.

Prayer is an especially emphatic form of symbolic-mythic communication. When we call on the "Spirit", we are using a word rich with implications. If we include the range of significance of the Greek and Hebrew words, spirit is clearly the power of all that lives. It is creative energy, breath, air, wind and tempest. Accordingly, Hübner speaks of the "mythic substantiality" of *pneuma*: "This word precisely expresses 'ideal-material unity' as a category of mythic thought" in a way that is impossible with the English words "spirit" or "ghost".[2] No wonder the statements in the hymn by Rabanus Maurus are so conspicuously elliptical.

This is why "pneumatology" represents a constant dilemma for theologians. It seems easier to talk about God or about Jesus as the Christ than to try to describe in doctrinal form a reality that encompasses us when we encounter it and evaporates as soon as we try to pin it down. "The wind [*pneuma*] blows where it chooses, and you hear the sound of it, but you do not know where it comes from or where it goes..." is how the gospel of John puts it (3:8). The presence of the *pneuma* cannot be captured by doctrinal statements. Instead we find approximations to it in such forms of symbolic interaction as prayer, song, ritual and sacrament. Encounters with the divine *pneuma* are beyond analysis and categorization. They are testified to, narrated, announced and disclosed.

To assert that appealing to the Creator Spirit can be understood only as a form of symbolic-mythic discourse but is yet meaningful runs counter to the widespread disregard for and ignorance of myth today. Myth is usually associated with primitive culture and thought and is considered outdated in view of the modern scientific understanding of the world. Believers, moreover, think of myth as the opposite of "truth" — lies and pagan error banished by the revelation of true religion.

Theological debate, especially in the German-language sphere, has not yet shaken off the repercussions of the "demythologization controversy" initiated by Rudolf Bultmann in 1941, which has had traumatic results, especially for grassroots piety, and has thus discouraged straightforward engagement with these issues.

However, philosophers like K. Hübner, H. Blumenberg and L. Kolakowski have shown that myth has an indispensable anthropological and socio-cultural dimension. Kolakowski, for instance, asserts that myth has an essential cohesive function in social life and an integrative effect in social organization not afforded by notions subject to scientific criteria. Myth, indeed, is not merely irreplaceable but has a constitutive role in all cultures and societies. It is at the basis of and interwoven with their forms of order and modes of thought and action. Kolakowski speaks of a "mythological energy" operating resolutely in every aspect of specifically human affairs, compelling us to put into words the essential content of mythic awareness. Of course we cannot ascribe the same cognitive meaning to such statements as we attribute to those formulated in empirical and rational contexts. We have to distinguish between the "mythological-symbolic" and the "technological-cognitive" functions of consciousness, even though certain "collisions" are inevitable. The vitality of any culture depends precisely on its being animated by a desire for an ultimate synthesis of its divergent elements and at the same time its "dynamic inability to achieve this synthesis".[3]

This is surely a decisive point. The vitality of a culture or religion is reflected in its "myth work". Its possibility of renewal is directly related to its readiness and ability to transform its particular dominant mythic traditions. Clearly this is a task for all sectors of a society, not only the religious.

Creation myths are often considered the typical form of mythic expression, with the forms of order of a particular society being those portrayed in its myths of origin. Although this is certainly true of many cultures, it does not exhaust the expressive capacity of myth. As we shall see later in looking at the biblical creation narratives, static creation myths can be transformed into dynamic historical myths.

The history of the last few centuries shows that myths can be formulated without any historical narrative material, in abstract form and in explicit contrast to established religious myths. Among these basic mythic formulas, as they might be called, are concepts such as "enlightenment" or "progress" or the idea of "Manifest Destiny" (which the United States has used to characterize its sense of mission) or the *Myth of the Twentieth Century* (Alfred Rosenberg's infamous legitimation of the absolute and sacred nature of Nazi ideology and practice).

There can be no real question of dispensing with myth. Any "demythologization" only prepares the way for a more or less explicit "re-mythologization". Instead, we should concentrate on promoting the creative and critical reworking of myth.

This also applies to the Christian religion. But the process is scarcely helped by forcing it into a false antithesis between serious theology and popular piety. Theological reflection, spirituality, worship life and Christian social action are all equally aspects of a transforming praxis and therefore testimonies and signs of a living and creative faith. Hübner rightly says that myth and religion are not the same, but whereas myth can be separated from religion, "there is no religion without myth".[4]

Our study of Rabanus Maurus' Pentecostal prayer has led us to an initial and summary examination of the meaning of the mythic mode. We have seen that it is fundamentally important for every religion and culture to be concerned with a creative transformation of its mythic basis; and, indeed, that the creative vitality of every religion and culture resides in that very concern.

I have already suggested that humanity is at an epoch-making transition-point. It is faced with the fundamental challenge of creatively transforming its cultural and religious goals and values. For humankind blindly to maintain its current cultural, scientific and economic paradigms will have catastrophic consequences for all life on this earth.

Rabanus Maurus' prayer should help us to contribute to this labour of transformation. When we invoke God's Spirit as Creator we acknowledge a fundamental and universal power and see our world in a new light. It becomes "creation", and thus acquires an axiomatic and essential dignity and value.

"Creation" is a mythic category. Accordingly it cannot be made interchangeable with terms such as "nature" or "universe". We can subject nature and the space roundabout our planets to scientific analysis and make them the object of systematic research. But creation is a category that preserves the inviolable subjectivity of all things, their ineradicably unique value and primordial status.

NOTES

[1] Cf. M. Buber, *I and Thou*, Edinburgh, 1937, p.14.
[2] K. Hübner, *Die Wahrheit des Mythos*, Munich, 1985, p.239.
[3] Cf. Leszek Kolakowski, *Die Gegenwärtigkeit des Mythos*, Munich, 1973, pp.148, 163, 166, 169.
[4] Hübner, *op. cit.*, pp.338, 344.

Chapter 2

God's Spirit:
The Basic Principle of Creation

"The Great Family"

The grey sea extends to the distant horizon. The waves roll in monotonously, rear up, abate and resume their onslaught. "How long has this been going on?", we wonder, but this goes on beyond time.

A sombre grey, taciturnly-clouded expanse of sky rises above the indifferent waters.

But the figure of a bird, a dove perhaps, reaches from the far horizon, high into the sky. Its tail touches the sea. It spreads its powerful wings upwards and across the sky. And wherever this dove extends its presence the sky is blue and sown with generous, airy clouds.

Is the dove rising? Or is it in fact descending? It is the great bird of life, opening up the heavens and hovering over the waters.

For me this painting by the Belgian artist René Magritte, entitled "The Great Family" (reproduced on the cover), is a mythic and visionary image of the moment at which creation began. The earth is without form and void. Darkness is upon the face of the deep and upon the waters. But the vital warmth of God's own light rises from the horizon in an immense gesture of benediction.

This is the *rûah* informing, fulfilling and opening up the heavens. Wherever her presence is felt, light and beauty prevail. This picture has helped me to understand better what the Bible means by *rûah*: the motherly energy of God, the inexhaustible and creative power that is exceedingly tender in the soft breezes and wondrously fierce in the tempest's blast. It is the breath, inspiration and soul of the world.

To be sure, what Magritte has portrayed here is only a faint reflection of this divine force which permeates all that is. But it is an energetic and hearty image, more expressive than the little doves suspended from the pulpit sounding-boards in many European churches. Even as a child I was not convinced by the pastor's solemn affirmation that this stiff dove a few centimetres above his head was the Holy Spirit, as important — so it was said — as Jesus (whose cross dominated the entire east end of the church) and indeed as God the Father himself (of whom no image could be made).

Perhaps this image retained from childhood explains why we can make so little of Pentecost as the feast of the Holy Spirit. What is there to honour and celebrate when the unique strength and power of the divine *rûah*, the fundamental life-bestowing force of creation, dwindles to the dimensions of an ineffectual dove (or, in more recent times, to the dove of peace, reproduced in a thousand different styles, many of them pure kitsch)?

Perhaps the rural people in the area where I grew up came closer to the truth when at Pentecost they decorated their houses and stables with fresh green birch branches. That was their symbolic attempt to introduce into their homes something of the breath of God, which was beginning once again to enliven nature with its special power, and to share in it.

Magritte's painting can help us to understand what the Creator Spirit is. Its emphasis on a few basic elements — water and primeval ocean, summer light and primordial bird — makes it a mythic image. "Mythic", because it tries to show the beginning, the first day of creation, as it were. I have suggested earlier that all cultures explore the origin of the world in mythic narratives, legends and songs. Myths are universal human categories that describe the presupposition of our presuppositions, the ground that transcends all forms of grounding.

To that extent, creation myths certainly have more to offer than information about the perennial question of where everything came from. While they speak about the beginning, they also seek to express something that is always valid. What was *in principio*, in the beginning, applies in principle. What was *en arche*, in the beginning, remains archetypical.

When Genesis 1:1 says, "In the beginning God created the heavens and the earth," this is much more than the introduction to an account of the origin of the world. The God who makes heaven and earth does so not only *in principio* but "in principle", so that no distinction can now be made between God and Creator. God is not known other than as the one who creates.

This is brought out in the Hebrew term for "make" or "create" — *bara*, which is used exclusively for God's generating activity. God's "making" is categorically distinct from all other kinds of making. The creations of God are the primordial and ultimate ground of all the creations of which creatures are capable.

Thus every statement about God is rooted in mythic discourse. But that does not mean that a myth must be repeated *ad infinitum*. As we have seen, it is characteristic of the vitality of the mythic approach to interpret and transform particular elements of myth. The first biblical creation narrative (Gen. 1:1-2:4a) is a prime example of this. This text, the product of priestly redactors, is a reworking of Egyptian and Babylonian myths. Two examples illustrate this:

• For the priestly author the verb *bara* means "utter", "make" and "name". Thus it should be clear that what God makes comes about in the uttering and naming of things, in the act of origination. Consequently these things themselves possess no divine power. Everything, as Psalm 19:1 firmly stresses, is the work of God's hands.

No matter how marvellous these works are, they do not merit any kind of honour in themselves, as if they were actually divine. Moreover, the words used have no sexual connotations. This creation myth allows no leeway for fertility cults, temple prostitution and similar abominations with which Israel's neighbours ritually interpreted the myth of the origin.

• Genesis 1:14-18 clearly demonstrates this iconoclastic interest. Whereas the Babylonians saw the sun, moon and stars as divinities, here these luminaries are demoted, so to speak, to the status of "lamps". Their task is to give light on the earth during the day and at night. Just that and no more. The uniqueness of Israel's God tolerates no star-divinities.

These two examples show that creative work on existing mythic material is not only possible but necessary for the sake of a new perception of the world. The priestly redaction reveals the transformative energy of the faith of Israel amidst the religious diversity of its time. The divinities are banished from the cosmos for the sake of a fundamentally new conception of God. For this reason the God of Israel is represented as the transcendent "maker". His image is given artisanal, monarchical, "scientific", technical and emphatically male characteristics. This accords with the understanding and perceptions of Israel we encounter in the Psalms, prophets and wisdom literature.

Exegetes like Gerhard von Rad and Hans Walter Wolff have taken great pains to demonstrate that ancient Israel "demythologized" the creation myths of its neighbours, in order to establish an enlightened historical view of God's work in the world and with God's people. In so doing they fall victim to the widespread understanding of myth only in terms of "stories of origin". Even if myths in many cultures take the form of narratives of origin, there are also myths which describe dynamic historical processes. A telling example is found in the myths of Israel, which set Genesis in close connection with the life of the patriarchs and, most notably, with the Exodus of the Chosen People from Egypt. What are often regarded as decisive epochs in the history of salvation are cast in mythic forms. The basic purpose is to present God not only as the source of original power but as an active leader of world affairs through and beyond Israel.

Hence Israel's search for Yahweh is "myth-work". And the Christian faith, although deeply rooted in this quest, is to be seen as a further dimension of "myth-work". I shall come back to this point in Chapter 7.

The priestly and scribal transformation of older mythic material proved fruitful for — indeed, essential to — the religious life of Israel and later the Christian church. Nevertheless, for many people today the creation myth in this form is no longer relevant. It has ceased to be a profoundly formative influence on our awareness of the world. God as a transcendent maker or leader can no longer be creatively reconciled with scientific findings about the origin of the universe. Not only women but men increasingly find the patriarchal emphasis of this image of God obsolete.

Such discrepancies show that the biblical materials have to be reworked in certain ways. This does not imply that the biblical text is to be discarded. What it does mean is that, as it encounters the varieties of contemporary experience, the archetypical power of the Bible can stimulate the production of new and appropriate images.

God and *rûah*

"The earth was a formless void and darkness covered the face of the deep, while the *rûah* of God swept over the face of the waters." This is how the mythic narrative begins. On closer scrutiny the terminology seems rather odd. Though "earth" is mentioned, it is not really earth but a ghastly void. The "deep" is also cited, but it is fathomless and resists any accurate verbal description. The suggestions of something hideous and horrific are reinforced by the mention of impenetrable darkness. All this is *tohu bohu*, chaos indeed.

Is the "*rûah* of God" part of the chaos described here? Westermann says yes.[1] The "divine *rûah*" is to be understood as a fearsome storm-wind over the waters, but not as the beginning of creation, not as that which "makes possible" the development of "primordial matter".[2] The creation proper begins instead with Genesis 1:3, with the "creative summons" that calls forth light. But whether or not we can find already in verse 2 a reference to the *rûah* hatching the primordial egg like a universal bird and preparing the creation, the interpretation is no different. For in verse 3, too, the closeness of *rûah* and God the Creator is constitutive.

God's "speaking" is generally interpreted as a monological summons. But to understand "Let there be light!" as a thundering command is a major misconception which has helped to keep our image of God within patriarchal confines. After all, *dabar*, divine discourse, is itself *rûah*-like. No speech is possible without breath. Breathing out is necessary to make sounds. Therefore the *rûah* is already present in God's first breath. It resounds in the first word. The etymological range of reference of the Latin *spiritus* includes the notion of "respiration". When God lives and breathes, and speaks and breathes out, respiratory processes begin.

Accordingly, we may understand "Let there be light!" as a slow, breath-taking and breath-expelling process of coming to be — as, indeed, a genesis. We must avoid any idea of God as a kind of electrician, switching on lights, in the way that floodlights suddenly come on above a stadium. We should think rather of a slow dawning process, of a gradual appearance and spreading of light, a process of *enlightening*.

Rûah, then, extends as God speaks, for God's speaking always includes action and process. Thus *rûah* creates the space in which life can unfold.

To put this in terms of trinitarian theology: the *rûah* emerges from God yet is equally original with God. Only because the *rûah* appears does God become alive and creative and thus meaningfully knowable as "Father". This supports the idea of what has been called *perichoresis* in Orthodox theology from John of Damascus onwards. God is not monadic but is to be understood as a "living fellowship of the three Persons who are related to one another and exist in one another".[3] This approach enables us to see God's speaking as a process of responding, of communication and exchange. In space and by virtue of this dialogical process, everything created acquires the dialogical and relational laws by which it endures. Thus all elements of creation reflect in their being the tension and potentiality that are in God. God's breath, *rûah*, is reflected in the respiratory processes of the cosmos.

Accordingly, Hildegard of Bingen speaks of the primordial power of creation as *viriditas*, the greening of the world.

In symbolic and mythic terms this means that as God breathes, the creation becomes ever more finely differentiated. As *rûah* is expelled, increasingly complex forms of life arise. The logical conclusion, both theologically and in evolutionary terms, is that human beings should be created at the end. They are created as man and woman, and are made thus "in the image of God". The female and male principles reflect the creative tension that is God. In those principles, as a result of human experience, we recognize God as Mother and Father and as the ground of all love. I would say that this inward tension of word and answer, of action and activity, also accords with the "us" that we find in verse 26: "Let *us* make humankind in our image, after our likeness." As was already shown, *dabar* implies a form of perichoretic communication. So the use of the first person plural is only another sign of God's "trialogical" nature.

Creation as pregnancy

Two questions constantly recur in the theology of creation. One is whether God "decided" on the creation or whether it should be seen as an "emanation" of the Deity. The other concerns the problem of *creatio ex nihilo*.

In regard to the former, I would observe here only that it essentially represents an attempt to reach behind Genesis 1 and ask the myth a question which it is not competent to answer. The biblical myth starts from the assumption that God discloses and makes himself known in *bara*. Accordingly, all we can know of God is what is imparted in this disclosure.

The notion of "emanation" seems to me to raise the problem of *creatio ex nihilo*. The question here is whether we may assume the presence of something outside God to be used as the material of creation. The theological answer has always been that God created everything *from nothing*. This answer clearly grows out of a need to stress the uniqueness and unconditioned originality of God, and to reject the participation of any other power in the world's origin. God is glorified as the sole origin of all being. Everything remains in the hands of God and returns to God. This is affirmed consistently, though the world may sometimes seem to be "with devils filled", in the words of Luther's famous hymn. The fissures that run through the world do not pass through God.

Yet we still wonder whether it is not necessary to conceive of a space outside God in which creation can occur? If God is all in all, is there any room left for creation?

Jewish theologians, especially Isaac Luria, proposed a solution with the *zim-zum* concept. According to this theory, God withdrew into himself in order to leave a space free outside himself — which was consequently "without form and void" — into which God could re-enter as Creator. God would then have made a "primeval space" outside God that would remain nothing as long as God did not fill it as Creator.

The idea is understandable, but its exposition remains abstract and artificial. I think we can find a more convincing solution to the problem if we approach it from a female, maternal angle. A pregnant woman prepares *within herself* the space for a living creature that is not herself yet draws its life from her. In this sense, it would be more logical to conceive of the "primeval space" of creation as a mother's womb.

Is there any reason to reject the idea of creation as a bringing forth for which the most appropriate analogy is that of the process of gestation within and delivery by a mother? Why should we not express the inexpressible concept of creation by recourse to the image of pregnancy?

Our human experience contains nothing more intimate, loving, creaturely and creative than this process of conception, bearing and bringing into the world. We can conceive of no relationship more intense than that of a mother with her unborn baby. That is true even though she knows that this child is another being, an individual, and will eventually even become a stranger. Why should we not think of the primeval space of creation as God's womb, and the process of creation as the process of gestation, in the sense that what we will eventually be has not yet emerged?

The fact that Hebrew uses the same word for "womb" and "mercy" is relevant here. The Hebrews were well aware that the protection of a mother's womb is the most profound and intimate metaphor for the mercy of God. They knew that the assurance which the creation intends to offer all living things should be depicted as something so intimate and obvious as the security we enjoy in our mother's womb, a sense of which we all retain in the feeling that we were once in paradise.

How would the people of the Hebrew Scriptures, who were so deeply conscious of this experiential analogy between the womb and the compassion of God, be liable to depict divine mercy? Surely the notion of the divine-maternal womb would at least form part of the way in which they expressed it.

Why then do we, especially men, find the association between creation and pregnancy odd and even improper? The main reason is probably that our image of God is still so exclusively male and manual and insufficiently erotic in emphasis. Within a tradition that has portrayed God as transcendent "Maker" and "Unmoved Mover", the images of human closeness which are inevitable in the metaphor of pregnancy seem too direct.

Moreover, this way of looking at creation could even imply its divinization, so that everything would share in the divine. The spectre of pantheism looms large.

But this objection can be met with the reminder that this is merely one specific way of stressing the divine origin of all creation. The Bible certainly affords a number of comparable "naturalistic" concepts. For instance, the Yahwist account of creation emphasizes that God has breathed soul and life into humankind. We need refer only to Psalm 33:6, Psalm 104 or Job 38:28ff.: "Has the rain a father, or who has begotten the drops of dew? From whose womb did the ice come forth...?" In Paul's address to the Athenians, we read: "Indeed, he is not far from each one of us. For 'In him we live and move and have our being'" (Acts 17:27f.).

Wolfhart Pannenberg has described the relations between God's Spirit and creation in terms proper to the field theories of physics,[4] which seems particularly apt because of their similarity to Stoic and early Christian concepts of the Spirit. In this connection he criticizes the *zim-zum* theory taken up by Moltmann, and emphasizes that space and time must always be related to "the space of the omnipresence of God".[5]

Expositions of the omnipresence and simultaneity of God are also wholly reconcilable with the notion of pregnancy. A woman is omnipresent to and absolutely simultaneous for her unborn child, and the relationship of God to creation can be seen in the same way.

Admittedly, the image of pregnancy suffers from a major disadvantage. Pregnancy necessarily includes a definite chronological conclusion and is not an end in itself. It has to issue in birth, and thereby the beginning of a new, independent life which constantly moves further and further away from the space of maternal omnipresence and "eternity". This very biological necessity makes it seem inappropriate to associate the image of pregnancy with the history of creation and its eschatological fulfilment. Pannenberg, to be sure, rightly emphasizes that "the function of the Spirit as originator of all life... appears as the preparation for the completion of his *activity in the bringing forth of new eschatological life*",[6] but we are not entitled to deduce from this the inevitability of creation history. We should rather recall the interpretative limits of all metaphor. As Pannenberg uses modern field theories to lend weight to the plausibility of creation as the action of the Spirit, so "creation as pregnancy" is a metaphor to illuminate the intimacy and selflessness of God's concentration on all creation, and to clarify the function of the space and time of creation within God's space-time. The same metaphor can also help to correct the unilaterally male tendency in our image of God, by allowing us to understand God's power as the omnipotence of love and not as the overbearing might of a potentate.

To return to Magritte's painting, we can now see why it is entitled *La Grande Famille* ("The Great Family"). The life of all creatures opens out in the dove's immense gesture of blessing, and everything proceeds from its light. Therefore everything is interrelated and forms one great family of life.

NOTES

[1] C. Westermann, *Genesis 1-11*, Neukirchen, 1974, pp.147ff.
[2] Cf. F. Delitzsch, quoted by Westermann, *ibid.*, p.151.
[3] J. Moltmann, *The Trinity and the Kingdom of God*, London, 1981, p.175.
[4] W. Pannenberg, *Systematische Theologie*, II, Göttingen, 1991, pp.99ff.
[5] *Ibid.*, p.110 n.229.
[6] *Ibid.*, p.120 (italics added).

Chapter 3

God's Spirit:
Fertility as the Original Blessing

Before saying anything about speaking, making and naming, the creation narrative in Genesis 1 describes *rûah* as offering the maternal womb of creation, the original space of life. Whatever comes to be in her sphere of influence shares in her life without being her, proceeds from her yet is distinct from her. It is potentiality and energy seeking form and shape.

Genesis 1 therefore assumes throughout that all kinds of life which come into existence are receptive, ready and *fertile*, each according to its kind. Grass and vegetation have seeds; trees surround their seed with fruits. The forms of life that dwell in the seas and the air are commanded to be fruitful and increase. Although this express summons may seem to be lacking in the account of the creation of the life-forms that are to inhabit the earth (cf. 1:24ff.), this divine commission always comes at the *end* of each "day" of creation. Since the work of the sixth day includes the creation of the man and woman, the first part of Genesis 1:28 — "be fruitful and multiply, and fill the earth" — also applies to the creatures of the earth. God's blessing here applies both to humans and to animals, and in a very basic way associates them with all other creatures.

Of course, the special position of humankind is announced in the further injunction to "have dominion" over other forms of life. In the second creation narrative this commission is unfolded in the command to "till" and "keep" the garden of Eden (Gen. 2:15).

Fertility: the blessedness of life
The blessing God bestows on all living things as they begin to exist comprises three interwoven aspects: fertility, propagation of the species and filling of the earth.

Although many men and women are not enthusiastic about the idea of fertility, not least because they have trouble enough with their own, we cannot ignore that it is proposed so straightforwardly, as a matter of course indeed, in the first few pages of Scripture. There is a good reason for this.

All forms of life, in their millionfold variations, live only because and as long as they are fertile. Indeed, they seem concerned only to maintain their particular species. Therefore, every living thing produces more progeny than are actually needed to preserve the species. Fertility is prodigal.

But this extravagance of the procreative instinct is no mere pointless whim of nature. It is the same abundant fruitfulness that God finds "very good", for it is the basis of the survival of other living creatures. Genesis 1:29 uses simple language to describe how living things need one another for sustenance. Today our knowledge of the interdependence of food chains and the reciprocal nature of the systems that make bacterial, vegetable and organic life possible is much more detailed. The "law of the jungle", the victorious struggle of strong against weak, is quite meaningful in an evolutionary perspective, though it is a ludicrously inappropriate description of our present situation. The jungle itself is no "green hell" but a marvellously sophisticated reciprocal framework of large and small organisms existing in delicately calibrated climatic conditions. Each element in these systems contributes to the survival of the others.

In this system procreation increases in accordance with an organism's weakness. The fewer natural enemies it has, the more complex and lower the rate of increase is. One need only compare the breeding behaviour of the salmon with that of the tiger to see the logic of these remarkable differences.

This is "very good" because the system is very good for all participants. Precisely because one's fertility is so unconditionally and radically intent on the propagation of one's own species, it produces an excess from which many other species are able to live. The life-cycles of birth and growth, maturing and dying are reciprocally supportive, and thus form the constantly changing yet extraordinarily stable life structures of the earth's ecosystems. It is precisely the abundance of fertility that forms the basis for the life of other organisms. Without this the history of nature in its various ecosystems would not exist. Of course this general harmony is associated with a great deal of individual suffering. Prodigal fertility always implies elements of pain and sacrifice.

The command to "fill the earth" forms a necessary part of the interdependence of all living things. From science we have learned more about this: that the deep ocean currents are decisively important not only for the climate of the continents but for marine life; that the tropical rain forests function as global lungs; that the earth's uranium had to disintegrate to a certain extent before the planet became safe for organic life.[1] These few examples testify that the earth is an interdependent system of ecosystems. The earth has to be "filled" with life so that each individual can enjoy its own little span of life. The impoverishment of any bio-region impoverishes all others. If the Amazon basin became a desert, it would have disastrous consequences for maintaining the oxygen and water equilibrium of the whole earth. If the polar ice-caps were to melt, certain ecosystems over the entire earth would be damaged.

Today, with the interdependence of the earth's ecosystems endangered, we know more about why reciprocal fertility, the procreative instinct and fulfilment of the earth are aspects of one and the same creative blessing.

This reciprocity is the basic vital embodiment of the essential potentiality of living matter. In mythic terms it is the indwelling of *rûah* in the "matter" of the cosmos. Therefore it is fundamentally important that our acknowledgment of the Spirit of God as the divine-maternal *rûah* should recognize the fruitfulness of all that lives. Our acknowledgment of the *Creator Spiritus* implies a conviction that the maternal-paternal love of God, God's concern for all creation, is unfolded in all creatures' urge to live, in their longing for survival and history.

Consequently we cannot speak of creation without affirming the original *blessing of fertility*. Ironically, the ecological crisis of our own time opens our eyes to this original blessing.

Human fertility

When speaking of non-human life, this idea of original blessing will seldom cause any difficulties. It is when we consider human fertility as an original blessing that a host of problems arises.

I said earlier that most women and men probably have certain inhibitions in this respect, because they experience their own sexual fertility as a burden and a problematical inheritance. For the most part they have to protect themselves from this particular "blessing", although no one wants to be infertile or impotent, for we know instinctively that fertility is a basic part of our being human.

We must remember that sexual fertility cannot be separated from the other vital and creative possibilities of our life. Modern psychology has shown us that from their very first breath all humans experience libidinous feelings and needs. At the same time, it is obvious that any uninhibited satisfaction of our sexuality is personally, socially and ecologically unsustainable. I have already mentioned that in the non-human realm the procreative instinct diminishes as the number of natural enemies decreases. Of course this must be even more true for the human species today, which has learned to defend itself against most natural enemies. Even though it is not the point here to discuss sexual ethics, it should be self-evident that the ordering and cultivation of fertility is one of the fundamental tasks of present-day human beings. This of course includes family planning.

Augustine's sexual pessimism is certainly responsible in part for the disappearance of the idea of the original blessing of the fertility of creation from the churches of the West and far beyond. To him we owe the notion that the procreative instinct is precisely the means of access to and the vehicle of original sin. Thus the basic creative pleasure which draws people together and without which no new human being, no nation and no history is conceivable — this sacrament of *rûah* — became the vehicle of sin. That this can be the case is incontestable. But Augustine's erroneous interpretation of it proved to be a fateful error in the history of the Christian church. *Original blessing* was turned into *original sin*. Joy in pleasure turned into pleasure as a burden; and fertility came to be seen as a matter of servitude and punishment.

This wrong turn by Augustine also led to a fateful division between God-as-Father and God-as-*rûah*, which subsequently proved impossible to repair. We might also call it the rift between creation and redemption. It is reflected in the separation of spirit and flesh, soul and body. This was the beginning of the "spiritualization" of the *Creator Spiritus*, which not only deprives the Spirit of vitality and substantiality, but makes what is bodily and material spirit-less and God-less.

This well-known separation appears in the human being's relation to his or her body. It has influenced the relation between the man, conceived of as the "head", and the woman, seen as the more "emotional, instinctive creature". It has deepened the gulf between humanity and the world. Where the Spirit is separated from the life of nature and the original closeness is abandoned, not only is God-*rûah* reduced to the stature of an ineffectual little dove, but nature is devitalized and robbed of its own dignity, and matter, the "maternal fabric" (as the Swiss writer Adolf Muschg puts it), is objectified to become raw material or mere resource.

In chapter 5 we shall look more closely at how we can speak meaningfully of "original sin". Here I want to enquire into the creative purpose of human fertility. To what extent can we ascribe to it what is said about the fruitfulness of all other creatures? Whereas these others procreate so prodigally yet support and make possible the life of other species, human beings behave differently. Humanity comes at the end of the food chain. It has hardly any natural enemies left. Things were not always so. At one time human beings were threatened by unforeseen changes of weather, famine, wild animals, diseases and epidemics. Thus large families were needed to preserve the species. Although many of these foes have been vanquished, there is still a kind of atavistic feeling that the world or nature is an enemy that we have to defend ourselves against.

Fertility and the mandate to have dominion

In earlier ages, the human commission to rule over nature could claim to be based on the need to ward off danger. But how are we to interpret this command today?

First we have to emphasize that this biblical blessing directs humans clearly and explicitly to the world of plants and animals. From the beginning, all human life is interlocked with that of other creatures. The basic elements of life are identical. Dependence on the earth's climatic conditions and the various ecosystems is unavoidable. It is characteristic of human beings, however, that they have also learned to establish themselves in the most unaccommodating of the earth's ecosystems, and thereby have indeed "filled" the earth.

But precisely this adaptation to the most varied of the world's bio-regions shows that human fertility is not merely a matter of blind procreative instinct, but consists in *shaping the world*. Thus, for example, the peoples of the Arctic wastes learned how to live in houses made from snow, to catch fish through holes in the ice and to construct a culture with what nature offered them. But that experience also included a strict insistence on family planning, which often also meant killing children. People in the tropics developed ingenious systems to build houses and gardens, and in the primeval forest they discovered important medicinal plants and herbs, even including some suitable for birth control. In the harsh procession of the seasons, other peoples learned to hunt, plough, farm, grow and cultivate. In all these processes of possessing and shaping the world, we may recognize the mythic meaning of "have dominion over".

The astonishing expressions of human creativity are no more than different forms of fertility. Human fertility is to be understood not only in a biological and sexual sense. We must also include its intellectual, artistic and manual aspects. Whereas all other forms of life have to be concerned only with the propagation of their species in order to fulfil their purpose on behalf of the whole, we humans have to conceive our fertility as a conscious and planned adaptation to the earth's life systems. Fertility means culture. That is the only thing that we as conscious organisms are in a position — and called — to add to the marvel of nature. We can transform nature into culture, but the goal cannot be a continual *replacement* of nature. Culture must always be conceived as an artificial *adaptation* to natural conditions of life.

The command to be fruitful and the commission to have dominion over the earth are ways of describing a task that only human beings can carry out: the transformation of natural conditions of life into cultural forms of life. C.F. von Weizsäcker expresses it this way:

> For animals the pleasure principle is the subjective expression of the unconscious, objective reality principle. In human beings the reality principle is explicit and results in the world of culture, which is not produced by and cannot be maintained by the pleasure principle. Asceticism has the cultural function of restraining the pleasure principle, and of maintaining the indicative function of suffering.[2]

Essentially, this cultural transformation of nature has succeeded to ever greater degrees only during the last eight millennia, which comprise but a moment in the history of the planet. At the end of the second millennium after Christ, however, it is plain that this transformation of nature into culture is on the verge of failure. The disappearance of so many species and the pollution of air, water and earth suggest that the capacity of *oikos* earth to bear human dominion has reached its limits. Thus the ecological crisis is also revealed as a crisis of our cultures, above all of Western culture.

This is a twofold concern: quantitatively, the earth cannot in the long run sustain an increased population at the present rates of growth; qualitatively, a minority of the world's population is taking far too much from nature and immeasurably overburdening it with poisons. At present one northern European represents as great an ecological burden as fifty Indians.

These well-known facts obviously constitute what in the present context amounts to a profound crisis of fertility. The population explosion is in many cases a desperate expression of the procreative instinct. The possibilities of cultural transformation cannot keep pace with it. It is a matter, therefore, of *culturally destructive procreation*. On the other hand, the exploitation of resources by rich societies has exceeded the bounds of what is ecologically feasible. Here it is a question of *culturally destructive consumption*. Procreation without order and consumption without reconstruction are both forms of uncontrolled "fertility" that betray the commission to cultivate and preserve. They do not fill the earth but empty it. They do not shape the fabric of life but tear deep holes in it.

The vision offered by the creation of a life in fullness for all thus presupposes a far-reaching new conception of human fruitfulness. The possibilities are clear. If the procreation and greed of the human species continue to advance as in past decades, truly large-scale ecological disasters are inevitable. Alternatively, we can rethink fertility and creativity as the shaping forces of this finite world, and self-preservation will become a function of self-control. We humans will be in harmony with the blessing of creation only if we make self-critical use of our empathic reason.

NOTES

[1] Thus it is contrary to the purpose of creation when the nuclear industry once again artificially releases this radiation energy, and does so to an extent unsustainable by organic life.

[2] In *Deutlichkeit: Beiträge zu politischen und religiösen Gegenwartsfragen*, Munich, 1978, p.87n.

Chapter 4

The Spirit of God
as Inexhaustible Power

"The Creation of Adam"

Michelangelo's "The Creation of Adam" is undoubtedly one of the most famous works of art in the Western world. Much has been written about its superb artistry. There are many interpretations of its portrayal of God's finger touching Adam's for the last time, the grave and solicitous look that God the Father gives him and the young Adam's still semi-conscious expression, full of yearning and pain.

Precisely because Michelangelo's painting is reproduced so often in textbooks, advertisements, post-cards and posters, it has helped to implant in the modern mind two fateful misunderstandings regarding God and the creation.

The first is that of a God with a long beard. What the artist intended as a symbol of maturity and wisdom has become an image of a God who has unmistakably reached old age. We are forced to ask: How long does he still have to live? Who will be the first to announce his death?

The other erroneous image has had even more serious consequences: creation as farewell. The picture quite clearly shows God departing once the human being he has made opens his eyes. With the creation of human beings — or, more precisely, of man — the work of creation is at an end. The Creator leaves with his retinue and returns to the heavenly heights. This is the moment when the man gets up and goes to his work. The old withdraws and the young takes over his labours. With the creation of Adam, God's work is finished. In the form of the human being a new subject is now on the scene to continue the work as a fully accredited deputy.

Michelangelo's painting confirms a widespread misconception of creation as only an event at the beginning. This fits in with a manual and technical notion of the creation as a vast machine, which the Creator made once long ago and set in motion, but which thereafter could carry on without him, under human guidance and control. In Christian theology this misunderstanding has also given rise to the assumption that the creation can be entrusted to its own laws, that its forms of life can be used at our own discretion and whim and that what really matters is God's "second" activity, the history of human salvation.

The Bible seems to support this misunderstanding by offering in the first few pages a summary account of the creation of the world, as if the intention is merely to set the scene for the unfolding of the real drama: God's struggle for human salvation. That is the sense of the traditional interpretations of salvation history, which reflect the cleavage between creation and redemption referred to earlier. Creation is the vast background for the great narratives that begin with the patriarchs, followed by the rescue of the descendants of Abraham from Egyptian slavery. Then comes the account of the colonization of the "promised land", achieved by means of "holy wars". Thereafter we have vivid accounts of God's faithfulness and Israel's apostasy, the remonstrances and consolation offered by the prophets, all the way to the traumatic experiences of exile and the destruction of Jerusalem. At this nadir in the fortunes of Israel, God's sacred drama provides a new beginning: with the advent of the only Son, a "new Israel" slowly comes into being and spreads over the earth. On the last day God visits his judgment on everything and makes a new heaven and a new earth.

Only in the last pages of the Bible, so it seems, do the saving work of God in Jesus Christ — the second Person of the Trinity — and the work of creation reunite. The work of creation culminates in the fulfilment of the work of salvation.

In Christendom concern about salvation is undoubtedly of more account than concern for creation. Creation is something taken for granted, or even opposed as inimical, as the "evil, sinful world". The salvation of one's soul is the focus of all possible energy. Indeed, our fundamental task is to do everything we can to obtain salvation. But we misunderstand this duty completely if it gives rise to a kind of "salvation-egoism" that regards the welfare and travail of creation as a matter of indifference.

The passion of the *rûah*: the kiss of life

By praying "Come, Holy Spirit" we seek to restore the association between creation and salvation. This prayer implicitly acknowledges our belief that no demiurge or alien spirit is at work in the world. The motherly *rûah* sustains all created things with its loving energy and thus unites the work of creation and the work of redemption.

To call the Spirit the "uncreated Power", as Paul Gerhardt does in a well-known hymn, comes close to asserting that the creation is not yet complete. The fact that the creation narrative repeatedly states that "it was good" does not imply a final judgment. Our examination of the nature of fertility has shown us that the "very good" of creation must be understood in terms of its character as process and its interdependent historicity.

God's *rûah* is the inexhaustible power which as the soul of the world bestows breath and order, energy and love of life on all things. It is the divine power that maintains creation, not in the way that an automobile has to be serviced regularly, but as the power that prompts the creation onwards because it has not yet reached its goal.

> These all look to you
> to give them their food in due season;
> when you give to them, they gather it up;
> when you open your hand, they are filled with good things.
> When you hide your face, they are dismayed;
> when you take away their breath ["Spirit"], they die
> and return to their dust.
> When you send forth your spirit, they are created;
> and you renew the face of the ground (Ps. 104:27-30).

God-*rûah* enlivens, ensouls and wholly governs everything that is. Accordingly, all things live by the original blessing of that abundant fertility which has its times and its occasions. Where the *rûah* draws in her breath, apathy and death prevail. Where the *rûah* is absent or concealed, we feel that profound fear which always assails us when the ground is taken from under our feet — a sense of terror familiar to people in earthquake zones. But where God-*rûah* issues forth with new strength the face of the earth is renewed.

"Thus God sustains the creation," says Gerhard Liedke, "by breathing with it, while it lives in his exhalation and inhalation."[1] Liedke uses the image of mouth-to-mouth resuscitation to bring out the intimacy of this process. Like the idea of pregnancy as metaphor for creation, this may also seem alien to some people, who would consider such an image of God's closeness to his creatures far too direct and even improper.

In Michelangelo's painting, the erotic aspect of the relationship between God and his creation can be detected, though in the restrained and sublimated way enjoined by official ecclesiastical morality. The second creation narrative of Genesis is more direct: "Then the Lord God formed man from the dust of the ground, and breathed into his nostrils the breath of life" (Gen. 2:7). Adam is given life, which means also a soul, through that intimate gesture known as the "kiss of life".

A male-centred church and theology have consciously weakened the force of this loving intimacy and passionate closeness, denying that this very "kiss of life" was the elixir of life of the *rûah*. Thus the *rûah* has been spiritualized, de-eroticized and rendered impotent. But if we do not take seriously this passionate aspect of the love which God allows, as it were, to impregnate the creation, it is impossible to understand the great travail of *creatio continua*, continuous creation.

Psalm 104 acknowledges something of the effort associated with the resuscitation and ensoulment of the world. From another angle, scientific investigation of the history of our planet has shown how consuming, laborious and immense is the continuous process of creation. The continents are ever in motion and the face of the earth is always changing. Ours is a living cosmos with an impressive history.

Fallen creation?

Behind the mythic term *creatio continua* lies a staggering confession. It is inconceivable that all this, which has taken thousands of millions of years to develop and will continue to unfold for thousands of millions to come, in which human history is but a moment, was and still is *creation*!

But it is not only its immeasurability that makes the ongoing creation seem so prodigious. The incomplete nature of creation also includes breaks and catastrophes. Volcanoes erupt and devastate entire towns and villages. But the volcanic soil that results from the lava flow is extraordinarily fertile. Volcanoes are necessary, for they release subterranean pressure. Earthquakes are terrifying but inevitable natural consequences of tectonic movements. The same is true of other natural disasters. They are signs that our planet is very much alive.

In its mythic and poetic style, Psalm 104 associates these processes with the inhalation and exhalation of the *rûah*. Here we finally realize how daring it is to acknowledge God as the Creator of heaven and earth. For it requires a certain audacity to recognize the frightful fissures that run through the history of the earth, such as the incalculable catastrophes that led to the extinction of the dinosaurs, as signs of the living activity of God-*rûah*.

All creation lives in the process of exhaling and inhaling, being born and dying, coming and going. It is evident, however, that the law of "eat and be eaten" is not only a good way of ensuring survival but also the source of unending suffering. And so we say "Nature is cruel!". Christian thought associates this experience with creation's "groaning in travail" and "bondage to decay", of which Paul speaks (Rom. 8:20-22). Consequently, we sometimes use the expression "fallen creation". But is the law of transience a sign of sin? Is the manifold suffering in nature an indication that it too is subject to God's anger?

I do not believe that the experience of finiteness and of suffering in nature justifies theological talk of a fallen creation. All creation lives and passes in the respiratory movements of the *rûah*. Living things fulfil their life's purpose in being born, growing up, procreating and dying. The "fall of Adam" has nothing to do with these terrible rifts and suffering. From the viewpoint of the history of the earth, it makes no sense to say that with human sinfulness nature also became subject to the fall. The savageness of nature, which often seems exceedingly cruel, existed aeons before the human species came into existence.

I believe we should have the courage to integrate the transience and suffering of nature into our image of creation. Although the harmony and beauty of creation give us every reason to celebrate God's benevolent power, as Haydn does so impressively in his oratorio *Creation*, this praise should not seek to mitigate or to suppress its violent and painful aspects. A belief in creation that wishes to remain realistic and sincere understands the vast process of "dying and becoming" (to use a phrase of Goethe's) not as sin but as blessing.

Then it must be clear that blessing always includes suffering, as we know from the twofold meaning of the word "passion". We have already seen that fertility always implies pain and sacrifice. Reverence for life at the level of created things includes readiness for sacrifice.

Therefore not all death is the "wages of sin" (Rom. 6:23), just as severity or ease of death is no yardstick of heavy or slight guilt.

Despite all personal anguish, the fact that all living things must die is not misfortune but a blessing.

The concept of death as sin is a soteriological category that can apply only to human beings. Only humans can intentionally and willingly misuse and destroy their own and other's lives. Accordingly, all people are victims and agents in a history of violence. We human beings go to our death in fear and terror, under the burden and in the shadow of this guilt. That is the price we pay for serving violent power.

Consequently, it is appropriate to say that creation suffers from the history of human violence, for it has to submit to the ways in which human beings exploit, pollute and lay it waste. It suffers from human fallenness, but is not itself fallen.

NOTE

[1] G. Liedke, *Im Bauch des Fisches: Ökologische Theologie*, Stuttgart, 1979, p.14.

Chapter 5

Sin as the History of Violence

Consciousness — a vacant place

When we cry "Come, Creator Spirit!", it is usually because we feel abandoned by all good spirits. We plead for God's strength because we are troubled by the force of evil powers.

Anguished questioning about the evil in the world is as old as the human race. Where does evil come from? How does it get into us? What is the source of its violent destructiveness?

There can be no satisfactory answer, for when we try to think about evil, sin or fate, we can do so only from within the boundaries of their power.

That is why the examination of the basis, origin and cause of evil assumes the same mythic character as questioning about the basis of life. Thus it is quite consistent for the Bible to include this problem among its myths of origin and to connect it directly with its accounts of the creation of humankind (Gen. 3). Myth associates the fall with the first human couple and thus makes clear that sin is an original problem of human history — but not of creation as a whole.

The mythical account tells us that the tempter is already lurking in the first doubt of the first human beings. Independent human will came into existence when it proved possible to conceive of an alternative (Should God not rather have said...?). And this volition is capable of following the twists and turns of its own way, right up to fratricide.

The mythic narrative in Genesis 3 places this discovery of our own potential in the serpent's mouth. Behind this story lie ancient aetiologies of which few traces remain today, which seek to attribute the origin of evil to a pre-personal or transcendental power. Yet the rest of the narrative shows quite clearly that God holds human beings themselves accountable. Their own ability to question, their consciousness, constitutes the vacant space into which evil can enter.

Henceforth God's power, which gives atoms their energetic tension and living things their tension-laden fertility, develops in humans as a form of tension in the conscious mind. Our consciousness is ultra-creative; it appears in the form of self-awareness, perception of the world and apprehension of God. This reflective capacity is the basis of the ability described earlier to shape the world as the specifically human form of fertility. At the same time it is the starting-point for self-destruction, the annihilation of the world and the obscuring of God's image. I see this as the very essence — or, rather, the nullity — of evil.

Reflection means rupture. It is the disruption of the matter-of-fact-ness to which all other living things are subject. It means the end of innocence and the beginning of guilt.

The potential which for me represents the original energy of creation becomes ambivalent in human consciousness. Only humans can praise God consciously: the stars can do so only in blind obedience. Human beings are therefore above all other created things and represent God's image in the world. But it is also characteristic of the ambivalence of the mind that humans refuse to praise God and disobey. This is the source of pleasure in rebellion, but also of anguish at the loss of innocence and of (self-) hatred because the unquestioned harmony of paradise is gone. The service of God and the murder of one's human kin are close to each other, as the myth of Cain and Abel (Gen. 4) makes evident.

Perhaps we may say that what we call sin is *poisoned consciousness* and *destructive fertility*. It remains God's energy, which is why it is so strong, but it is perverted to the point that we take the law into our own hands. It is the spirit of God, but it is, in Luther's words, "misshapen" and turned to destructive ends.

And so, despite all its destructive potential, sin remains under God and is thus open to forgiveness.

Original sin and original blessing

The essence of evil is destructive energy, power turned to violence, polarity transformed into dualism. Consequently, human history always unfolds as the history of violence. We are all born into it; it is our heritage, whether we want it or not. In this sense we can speak of original sin quite apart from any biologistic notion that sin is transmitted through concupiscence. By growing up and developing a conscious mind, we become part of that history and continue it. The history of wrongdoing is also our history; it is our action as well as our fate.

To talk about original sin like this is not of course to imply that the original blessing is cancelled. Humankind is fallen. In the words of Luther's hymn: "Through Adam's fall/ We cannot choose,/ A fatal gift we merit:/ The taint we all/ Would try to lose/ But by our birth inherit." Still, this does not mean that human beings fall from their created state or are handed over to some dualistic demiurge. God-*rûah* remains our breath and soul. We experience the evil in the world as our own anguish. For that very reason the creation remains creation and the original blessing remains in force.

Since the point here is not to develop a "doctrine of sin", it is not necessary to describe in detail what sin is capable of. For that we need only look at the daily newspaper. I shall merely refer to some aspects of the subject.

As destructive energy, sin turns people against themselves. How much energy is expended on envy, greed, hatred and jealousy! How much effort is needed in life when we fall out with ourselves! How much violence we do to ourselves when we are dependent or in bondage, embittered or enraged! When we sin, we sacrifice ourselves first.

In addition, of course, we turn our destructive energy onto other people in the form of violence, whether in the covert form of manipulating their thoughts and feelings or in the more obvious forms of child abuse, violence against women, violence against weaker individuals or subject nations or cruelty towards animals. The abuse of power becomes domination, turning fellow-creatures into sacrifices and prey. The bloody traces of the history of violence can be seen in campaigns and wars (including "holy wars"), crusades, pogroms and conquests, but also in "marketing strategies" and trade wars, unjust economic relations and other forms of exploitation.

All too often nowadays, however, we experience another form of destructive energy: violence against animals and plants has become the global exercise of violence against the earth itself. It is not only what Eduardo Galeano calls "the open veins of Latin America" that testify to this history of violation of nature. The same silent cry rises from polluted rivers and lakes, lands and seas.

These few instances of the violence of sin show that it can and does corrupt and erase entire relationships essential to our lives.

These include sexual relationships but others as well. Too often the church has looked far more severely on sexual misdeeds than on many other acts that are no less destructive — for example, in the realm of business, trade or politics. It is not only sexual violence that offends against the blessing of fertility, but also economic and political violence; indeed, economics and politics are the most powerful ways of manipulating and destroying the world.

But we must go a little further and seek out the element of violence in reflective thought itself. We encounter this wherever the creative polarity that permeates the fabric of creation is rent into dualisms. It is the case, for example, when nature is seen only as an object of human intervention. This objectifying approach has a violent character, not least in the increasingly sophisticated forms of scientific research.

If we find the methodological dualism of science violent, we must not forget the surely no less violent expressions of religious dualism. Here too a rift is made where polar tension should be preserved. Religious dualism separates creation from salvation, divides the peace of the soul from peace in and with all that lives, marks traditions and convictions as sectarian absolutes and demonizes other religions as infidel creeds. The various fundamentalist tendencies have a common root in this dualism.

With the triumph of modern science and technology, this dualistic way of thinking and acting has become global. Modern global civilization is characterized by violent treatment of the planet.

Sin against the Spirit: the return of chaos

Earlier in this chapter we spoke of sin as destructive fertility, consciousness turned violent. We also noted that sin remains under God, just as the creation remains under the Creator. So the Bible is full of stories, sayings and songs which affirm that God loves to forgive the sins of human beings. God "forgives all your iniquity..., heals all your diseases", says the Psalmist (103:3). Forgiving is one of the ways in which God remains the Creator, restoring the brokenness and healing the wounds caused by human sin. And yet there is one sin, the gospels say, that cannot be forgiven, the sin against the Spirit (Matt. 12:31f. and parallels). About this enigmatic passage there has been a great deal of speculation.[1] I would like to suggest that the unforgivable sin would be to do away with the Spirit itself — to undo creation, as it were — and that humanity has reached a point in its history at which such an horrific act has become possible. A large nuclear war would probably destroy all life-forms on earth. But we must also consider the possibility of ecological disasters that could destroy the respiratory processes on which all life depends.

Of course, the death of created things does not imply the death of the *rûah*. But the memory of it would be lost. The word would be silent. God's breath would suffocate. Nothing would remain but the darkness covering the face of the deep (Gen. 1:2) and the Spirit of God sweeping over a burnt-out earth. But the "still, small voice" of God's presence would be dead. No one would be there to ask or need forgiveness. And there would be no one who could forgive, for forgiveness can come only through the victims and with even the memory of the victims gone, sin itself would become null and void.

Obviously, this explanation does not figure among the classical interpretations of Matthew 12:31ff., for it would have been incomprehensible before our time. But as we face the annihilative powers of humanity, such an exegesis should be admitted.

This points us to the demonic nature of sin and violence as revealed in the unprecedented destructive power of our times. Humanity has turned against the earth itself. It is intent on destroying the very ground from which it was taken. As Thomas Berry observes, "We are the affliction of the world, its demonic presence".[2] Such an ecocidal — and at the same time suicidal — undertaking would be the culmination of destructiveness. It would mean the return of chaos.

For just as the creation should be understood as more than an initial event, so chaos should not be taken as something definitively past. Chaos is tamed by creation. It is, so to speak, permanently held down by the *creatio continua* and permanently transformed in a productive sense. But this also means that chaos is still there. Here, too, a myth from the first pages of the Bible has something to tell us. The power of chaos invades Cain in his anger with his brother and his bitter vexation at the rejection of his sacrifice. In Genesis 4:7 God himself warns Cain of the danger that threatens him: "Sin is lurking at the door..., but you must master it!" This "mastering" refers to the same ordering power that I described as creative shaping of the world. But Cain loses this self-controlling power and allows the "serpent" to slip into his house. Chaos returns and deafens Cain to God's warning and conciliatory word. And thus Abel must die. The voice of his blood crying out to God is the living breath by which the *rûah* dwells in all its children. This is the voice with which it accuses the murderer.

The myth teaches us that this fratricide did not happen once upon a time in the grey mists of prehistory but is our present condition. It happens again and again. Chaos, the nullifying and annihilating power, is lurking at the door to interrupt the advance of life.

The myth of the flood is also a description of the return of chaos. When Genesis 6:5ff. tells us that God could no longer tolerate the wickedness of humankind, it reveals a moment of abysmal horror. What is bound to happen when God gives up caring for creation, when God's love is swept away by sorrow? Then all dams break, all flood-gates open. Then chaos once again overwhelms the world.

The myth of the great flood can thus be taken as a counterpart to the myth of creation. It shows what happens when God's energy is drowned in anguish. Chaos returns.

The haunting reference in the gospels to the unforgivable sin against the Spirit is a reminder that the annihilative power of human violence is not to be taken lightly. The myth knows that chaos is just waiting for an opportunity to strike at life itself. In our own time, the images for the return of chaos include not only the flood but above all the nuclear firestorm and the global winter.

Flood, plague, fire and darkness are mythic images that haunt our story. They reveal the transpersonal nature of sin: power without love, energy without spirit, turning the world into deserts and wastelands.

NOTES

[1] For a discussion see, for example, the classic commentary on Matthew by U. Luz, *EKK*, 1/2, Zurich and Neukirchen, 1990, pp.256-71.
[2] *The Dream of the Earth*, San Francisco, Sierra Club Books, 1988, p.209.

Chapter 6

Jesus of Nazareth: God's Spirit in Person

The essential Word

How are we to relate the life and work of Jesus Christ to the original work of creation? The New Testament offers two approaches, which we may call the *cosmological* approach and the *salvation-history* approach.

We encounter the former in the Johannine writings. The *logos* that was with God before all times becomes human in Jesus of Nazareth. The same energy that summons the creation into being and maintains it in existence is personified in the activity, suffering and death of this person. No Spirit other than the one active in creation is active in him. The *rûah*-God is one and the same, on "the first day of creation", on each day, and as it were *in person* in this Jesus.

The cosmological interpretation of the mystery that is Jesus describes a vast arc between this individual human being and the essential ground of all life. The unifying principle is what the Hellenistic world knew as *logos*, the energy proper to all life and uniting all life. This approach is cosmological also because it conceives the mission and activity of Jesus as serving the cosmos: "For God so loved the world [*cosmos*] that he gave his only Son" (John 3:16). The goal of the Son's mission extends through the salvation of humankind all the way to the redemption of creation.

The salvation-history approach is found in Matthew and Luke. Matthew begins his gospel with a genealogical presentation with three times fourteen generations, starting with Abraham, marking decisive events in the history of Israel, passing through Joseph and culminating in Jesus. From the very outset, he makes it clear that the history of God and his people which began with Abraham, the "father of faith", has its decisive point and fulfilment in Jesus. Yet there is no mention of the cosmos in this covenant-based concept of salvation history. Humanity is at the centre, as it is in the programmatic conclusion of the gospel (Matt. 28:18ff.).

Luke's approach is different. He also offers a genealogy (3:23ff.), but takes it back from Jesus through Joseph to Adam and to God himself: "...the son of Adam, the son of God" (3:38). Here the historical line of the covenant mentioned by Matthew is given a universal frame of reference. By means of his genealogy, Luke traces the course of salvation history back from Jesus to God, and thus connects the Christ-event with the creation. The very next words we read are: "Jesus, full of the Holy Spirit..." (4:1). This is the beginning of Luke's temptation narrative (once again stressing the power of the *pneuma*), which then moves on to the history of Jesus' mission (cf. 4:14ff.).

A revealing association of these two types is found in the letter to the Hebrews. Here too the fundamental approach is that of salvation history, but it does not take a genealogical form. A basic perspective of Jewish belief is central here: the history of the proclamation of salvation through the prophets, which comes to an end with "the Son". This perspective is then given a cosmological emphasis: this is the Son through whom God made the world, who upholds all things through his word of power, and is therefore the "heir" who is the "reflection of God's glory" and bears "the exact imprint of God's very being" (1:2ff.). It is abundantly clear that the proclamation of this Jesus of Nazareth, indeed his life up to his death and resurrection, is associated with God's creative activity. The Word through which God built the house of earth takes on our human life. The radicality of this adoption of human flesh is made fully evident in the self-sacrifice of death on the cross. Hebrews 9:14 underlines that this sacrifice was offered "through the eternal Spirit". The Son culminates and fulfils his self-emptying, his *kenosis*, by entering the depths of death. In this way — and this is the mystery — is manifested the power that undermines and will ultimately defeat the entire history of violence. By accepting suffering and death in an act of absolute self-emptying, Jesus is upholding the universe by his word of power (cf. 1:3). That is vouched for in his resurrection.

This identity of creative and messianic power is fundamentally important. We encounter it constantly in the theological discussions of the early Christian communities — the best-known example being the formulation of the Nicene Creed that Jesus is "God of God" and "light of light".

Another aspect has to be taken into account here. The four evangelists agree in reporting the baptism of Jesus and his ensoul-

ment by the *pneuma*. The Christian church has always understood baptism as a new birth, as birth through the *pneuma*. Thus
the baptism of Jesus marks his new coming-to-be, because God
the Spirit ensouls him and gives him life. Baptism and the gift of
the *pneuma* therefore represent a further aspect of associating
Jesus' life and activity as closely as possible with the life and
activity of the entire creation. The inner logic of this is seen in the
fact that Jesus' activity takes place by virtue of the same power
which in the beginning — so to speak, in the first exhalation of
God — produced light. *Rûah* and *pneuma* are one and the same
power.

The image of the Son

The genealogies mentioned above show that the first Christian
communities used the language of biological causation to express
the oneness of their Messiah with the creative power that is the
ground of everything. Since Jesus himself expressed his closeness
to God by using the intimate word "Abba", the image of the Son
was an obvious choice. Thus Jesus came to be spoken of as "Son
of God" or "Son of the Father". Feminist theologians have
insisted that we should talk of Jesus as the Son of the *rûah* or of
sophia (wisdom).[1] It is significant that Syrian Christians spoke of
the *rûah* as Mother.[2] This point is very relevant for overcoming
any restrictive patriarchalism in our understanding of the relationship between Jesus and God.

In chapter 2 I described all creation as taking place in the
breath of God. This divine creativity is merciful and erotic
because it seeks its pleasure in all created things. I proposed the
image of the maternal womb to indicate how the history of life is
hidden in the original space of God's lovingkindness. Consequently, I suggest that, rather than replacing patriarchal images of
God with female images, it is more appropriate to use images of
parental relationships. A critique of patriarchalism is certainly
important, but it should not lead to a new dualism.

Images of parental relationships preserve the quality of the
polar context and indeed necessarily lead beyond to triadic concepts, for parents apart from their children are only a couple. The
child alone conveys the status of parenthood. In this perspective,
we would have to see Jesus as the Son of the Father and of the
Mother. In the language of trinitarian theology, he proceeds from
the Father and from the (female) Spirit. But by being the child, he

reveals for the first time the fatherhood of God and the mother-hood of the *rûah*.

The *logos* as liberator

For whom did the life, crucifixion and resurrection of this Jesus happen? Clearly the New Testament has no exclusively anthropological salvation in mind. Jesus is described as the new Adam, the first fruits of the new creation (cf. 1 Cor. 15:20ff.). He must rise from the dead because in him is manifest the new human being, in whom the divine creative energy and love are alive.

In all things he was as a human being is, the letter to the Hebrews insists, but "without sin" (4:15). Interpreting these words along the lines of what was said about sin in the preceding chapter, the energy of creation is present in Jesus *without its destructiveness and addiction to chaos*. The demons are the first to acknowledge this. As representatives of chaotic-destructive forces in human beings, they recognize, as it were "instinctively", that the advent of this anointed one means that their own end has come. That is why people who are sick or suffering from other afflictions want his healing power. That is why the guilty, like the thief on the cross, seek his comforting presence. That is why people who are in the shadow of death follow him, for they sense that he is their liberator. Women above all, disadvantaged and despised by the dominant culture and religion, recognize in him a new way for women and men to live together, a new dignity and joy.

The traces of the new world are apparent in all these forms of expectation and discipleship. The power of the new creation is revealed in the miracles of the Messiah; they are a foretaste and down-payment of the life that is opened up with the resurrected Lord. God becomes a human being, not because God is indifferent to the other forms of creation, but because it is we humans who sinned and thus became the great destructive element of creation. Human beings need liberation in order to live lives of service to creation. Human beings need redemption so that once again they can serve creation in freedom.

In his sermon of 12 May 1538, Luther says: "Was Christ born for the sake of geese, cows and pigs? No, he became a man. If he had wanted to help the beasts, he would have taken on the shape of a cow."[3] Such an anthropocentric misunderstanding of salvation, as though God is concerned only with human beings and

uninterested in geese, cows and pigs, has undoubtedly contributed to the abuse of other living creatures as mere "beasts of
burden" and "breeding stock".

Luther's words should rather be understood in conjunction
with Jesus' pronouncement: "Those who are well have no need of
a physician, but those who are sick" (Luke 5:31). The geese, cows
and pigs are "those who are well", in the sense of living in
accordance with God's commandments. Human beings, however, can behave differently, because they are the part of creation
endowed with consciousness and an ability to make decisions.
Mortally sick in this respect, they need a doctor.

This interpretation is reinforced by another saying attributed
to Luther: "The sun does not shine on its own account, or the
water flow for its own sake. Similarly all creatures obey the law of
love and their whole nature lives in the law of the Lord... Only
the designs of the [human] heart are wicked. They seek only their
own ends everywhere, even in respect of God." Here humanity is
identified as the fallen part of creation which has perverted the
"law of love". That is why Christ became human. Because
humankind is in profound danger and has in the process become
profoundly dangerous for all of life, God's *logos* comes to its aid.

Therefore Jesus is concerned with salvation from sin, that is,
with liberation from the violence that destroys all relationships
and, in a positive sense, with the restoration of the peace of
creation.

Here again we may refer to what was said about *creatio
continua*. In Jesus the liberator, we realize that this concept
receives its full meaning only in a Christological context. *Creatio
continua* can be seen as permanent resistance to the forces of
chaos; Jesus' acts of healing, his preaching and his cross are
properly understood in the same terms. When the gospels say
Jesus drove out demons and evil spirits, they are giving exemplary
and symbolic expression to his resistance to the devastating power
of chaos.

We should understand his death similarly. His suffering is no
cowardly silence but a standing up to the powers of darkness.
Hebrews 9:14 emphasizes that Christ offered himself up on the
cross "through the eternal *pneuma*". This sacrifice shows the cost
of persisting in the work of creation.

Persisting, standing firm and abiding — the literal meanings of
the Greek word for patience, *hypomone* — go together. The trials

and temptations in Gethsemane show that this patience is not to be taken for granted. Jesus' fear and hesitation reflect something of God's grief before the flood. But no flood follows here, and no fiery judgment, but the bearing of evil right up to death on the cross.

Since the first Good Friday, Christians have honoured the cross of Christ as the unsurpassable sign of love, as the bulwark of mercy with which God holds on to creation through the eternal *rûah*. It is the basic symbol of the new covenant set in the midst of human history. By this means God comes "in our flesh" and his love is with us. It is more concrete than the sign of the rainbow which God placed in the clouds after the flood (Gen. 9:12ff.). Thus Jesus of Nazareth is the God-Spirit in person, the seal of the peace of creation.

The *logos* as child of the new creation

We noted above that the gospels all report that Jesus uniquely called the one God "Abba". While this is usually translated "Father", it was in fact the familiar form of address used by children. Jesus' relationship with God was intimate to a degree previously unknown. While pious Jews hesitated out of sheer respect and reverence to use any name to address God — could there be any names at all for Yahweh? — this Jesus addresses the Almighty in the most childlike and trusting way. He breaks through the distance and strictness of God, the Ruler of heaven and earth. The only person who can speak like that is someone who lives in the innocence of paradise — or, better, as "the first freedman or freedwoman of the new creation".[4]

This tender straightforwardness, a prime feature of Jesus' understanding of his relationship with God, characterized his own treatment of children.[5] Jesus was not someone who just doted on children. He saw their directness and simple trust as a powerful symbol of the trust he himself embodied and wished to implant in his disciples.

That is why the idea of a child's relationship with its parents plays such a major role in Paul (cf. Rom. 8:17; Gal. 4:6ff.). The followers of Jesus did not "receive a spirit of slavery to fall back into fear" (Rom. 8:15). Staying close to this Child and Heir, Jesus' disciples also become children and heirs with him, and thus "a kind of first fruits of his creatures" (James 1:18).

Thus what we are to be was made apparent in Jesus. As the resurrected Lord, he put off this perishable nature and "put on imperishability" (1 Cor. 15:53). In this new embodiment he makes himself present to his own. He reveals himself to them as the one who leads them forward; in other words, he opens up a new space and a new time for them. That is the dimension in which his mission is accomplished.

If with Paul we understand the resurrection as the revelation of the new creation, we find yet another link with the idea of "creation as pregnancy". When we think of Christ as the child of the *rûah*, and thus as the first fruit, the new Adam, in whom we see that which all are called to become, Easter can be conceived in a profoundly symbolic sense as the beginning of a new creation.

The first Christian communities clearly lived with the energizing certainty that a new age had dawned on the morning of the resurrection. By baptism they were born into this new creation. As people of this new age they could take on the persecutions of this passing time and its violence without betraying their mission. Only in this perspective can we understand the history of the mission of the first few centuries of the Christian era, which was always a history of martyrdom. When the resurrected Christ is seen and believed in as the first child of the new creation, eschatological hope can take root: hope in a world in which justice and peace finally embrace. This resurrected Lord is the child that proceeds from the Father and the *rûah*. He shows the world its own promise; he reveals the very ground by which it has always been supported.

Childhood and covenant

We have seen that the way in which Jesus addressed God was entirely new to the Jewish people. This relationship with God also modifies the understanding of the covenant with which his people sought to express their relationship to God. By disclosing and bestowing on humankind the status of child of God, Jesus gives relationship to God a closeness and immediacy that are foreign to the idea of the covenant as found in the Hebrew Scriptures. To be sure, the covenantal sequence from Noah through Abraham and Moses to David testifies to Yahweh's loyalty to the covenant, but it also indicates a certain distance, in which it is always quite clear who is "the Highest". The relationship always depends on the law of the covenant, and is a permanent struggle between duty and disobedience. There is no room for the kind of relationship a child has with its parents.

The fundamentally problematical nature of the covenant idea was made clear by Jeremiah, who looks forward to a time when the law of God will enter the heart and mind of the people, and thus no longer remain distinct from the thinking and considerations of the human heart (cf. 31:3ff.). When this is second nature, the covenant is fulfilled, because it is cancelled. When the full union of God's will and the human will has been attained, the covenant will be superfluous, for something new will have occurred, namely, *incarnation*.

Christians see what is promised by Jeremiah as fulfilled in the flesh in Jesus Christ. He is the incarnation of the nature and will of God. In him the loving, creative *rûah* is personified. The covenant relationship between the Almighty and humankind has become the relationship of a parent and a child. The distance has been cancelled.

Christians have always believed that the *pneuma* of this child-parent relationship of Jesus was transmitted to his disciples. As limbs of the body of Christ, they share in the directness and freedom of the children of God. They too live with the promise of being freed men and women of creation. Of course this is a profession of faith despite all appearances, a hope contrary to everyday experience.

The message that sinners are justified by grace alone is one way of expressing the concept of being a child of God. This view maintains that no covenant law can produce obedience but that our just behaviour must proceed from a transformation of our being. The bestowal of grace includes the unprecedented assurance that the Spirit of Christ will unite with our thought and endeavours. Then we try to conduct our lives in accordance with the Spirit of God, not because of compulsion of any kind but of our own free will.

Of course we must also consider the other side of the message of justification, which realistically takes into account the ongoing power of sin in the life of believers and acknowledges that no earthly law can protect us from the inevitable attractiveness of sin. Only a constantly renewed existential conversion allows us to oppose the history of violence and evil. Each day, ever and again, we have to overcome the misfortune of our dependence by virtue of the enlivening power of the divine *pneuma*. Only thus do we become explicit custodians of creation.

The most radical expression in Christian theology of this aspect of a fundamental change through the Spirit of Christ is the Orthodox notion of *theosis*, the idea that God became human so that we should become God. This concept has always been deeply imbued with the implications of creation theology. Only a humanity that begins to live from God's *rûah* is once again enabled through Christ to live in the likeness of God. Of course, humankind still remains part of the created world, but now it has been set free to work for the peace of creation.

NOTES

[1] Cf. C. Mulack, "Der Weg des Weiblichen ans Licht des Bewusstseins Jesu", in *Die Weiblichkeit Gottes*, 2nd ed., Stuttgart, 1983, pp.263ff.

[2] Cf. J. Moltmann, *The Spirit of Life*, London, 1992, pp.157ff.

[3] I am grateful to the Luther Archives of the Institute of the Late Middle Ages and the Reformation of the University of Tübingen for this reference.

[4] Cf. J. Moltmann, *Die ersten Freigelassenen der Schöpfung*, 2nd ed., Munich, 1971 (translated into English as *Theology of Play*).

[5] Cf. H.R. Weber, *Jesus and the Children: Biblical Resources for Study and Preaching*, Geneva, 1979; G. Müller-Fahrenholz, *Jesus von Nazareth: Gottes Kind — Bruder der Menschen*, Hamburg, 1991, pp.3-6.

Chapter 7

Alpha and Omega

In Albenga, Italy, a baptistery built in the late fifth century was decorated with a mosaic whose precision of style and expression are impressive.

The principal motif consists of three concentric circles on a dark-blue background. The innermost circle is light-blue; the middle one somewhat darker; and the outermost dark blue, almost as dark as the background itself. The Greek letters *chi* and *rho* in bright gold are discernible on the inner circle. They represent the name of Christ and have since the earliest days of Christianity symbolized belief in Christ as King and Lord. This Christogram extends over the middle and outer circles so that ultimately it dominates the entire surface of the design.

Between the two arms of the "X" are the Greek letters *alpha* and *omega*, also in gold. These two letters also reappear, slightly enlarged, in the two outer ovals.

Twelve doves, standing for the twelve apostles, are arranged around the central design in a lifelike and unforced manner, facing the threefold circle.

All this is set in a framework of green tendrils and cruciform leaves on a white ground — a reference to the Garden of Paradise. Four stars appear in the corners of the mosaic, symbolizing the cosmic extension of the central imagery.[1]

The Albenga mosaic is a pictorial version of faith in Christ as the *kyrios* of the world. The cosmic field of reference is clear: Christ is the Ruler of the universe. The threefold imposition of the circles and the monogram stress their Trinitarian implications, as does the repetition of the Alpha and Omega. The whole presentation is framed and, so to speak, supported by the twelve apostles.

The basic symbols of the Christian trinitarian myth which I recognize in the Albenga mosaic bring me back to my introductory remarks in chapter 1.

Paul Tillich says: "No myth can be created, no unity of the rational functions can be reached, on the basis of reason in conflict. *A new myth is the expression of the reuniting power of a new revelation*, not a product of formalized reason."[2] When the Albenga mosaic was created, the dogmatic and expository interpretation of the revelation that had entered the world with Jesus of Nazareth had reached its first major culminating point. To use an expression of H. Blumenberg, we might call this process of reflective interpretation a vast enterprise of "myth work".[3] Exactly what does this mean?

Sketching with broad strokes, we might say that in the first four centuries the dogmatic treatment of the Christ-event had to solve two fundamental and concentric problems: Christology and Trinitarian theology.

In essence the Christological questions centred on finding an appropriate account of the relationship between Christ's divine and human "natures". On the one hand, this was prompted by critical opposition to polytheistic images of God and the philosophical traditions of peoples and cultures in which Christian belief was taking root, especially the widespread gnostic tendencies of the period. On the other hand, the development of Christology involved confrontation with the beliefs of the Jewish people. How was the relation of this Christ to the God of Israel to be understood? How were the gospel of Jesus Christ and the great literature of the Jewish people related?

These questions could be worked out only within the setting of Trinitarian theology. I believe that is why this theology became so decisively important. The concept of the Trinity made it possible to express the universal significance of the revelation of Jesus Christ and to associate it with the traditions of the Jewish people. The God of the Jews and the God of Christians are brought together as "Father" and "Son". The "work" of the Father and the "work" of the Son are conjoined in the same way. The *rûah*, also known as *sophia* or *shekinah*, is understood as the divine power that defines and accompanies Jesus' life from the beginning. The creation of the world, the covenant with Israel and the redemption of all humankind in Jesus Christ are not separate processes; they are fundamentally related and indeed inconceivable apart from one another.

The Yahwist account of creation describes Adam's quest for the being appropriate to him, for the "thou" that can accord with him (Gen. 2:20ff.). He does not find it in the animal world. Only in Eve, his human counterpart, does he discover the creature in whom he recognizes his own flesh and blood, his nature and his quest: "This at last is bone of my bones and flesh of my flesh; this one shall be called Woman" (2:23).

Perhaps it is not so far-fetched to draw an analogy here with the voice from heaven at Jesus' baptism: "You are my Son, the beloved; with you I am well pleased" (Mark 1:11). Not only does this acclamation authenticate Jesus in the eyes of his disciples but also (to use the somewhat ingenuous language of myth) it offers decisive evidence of divine parenthood. In this Jesus of Nazareth God discovers his "Thou", whom he has sought throughout the entire creation. In him God recognizes his own nature. The Word that was with God in the beginning returns to its origin in the word lived and testified to by this Son of man.

In this one the meaning of creation history reveals itself as God's quest for "our image, according to our likeness" (Gen. 1:26). Jesus enables us to understand this history not only as the activity of God's abundant love but also as love in search of love. God wants to be loved. That is his "loving kindness", his joy. This loving kindness finds its focus in the child who so tenderly and trustingly calls God "Abba".

The *rûah* or *pneuma* plays a central role in the structure of this relationship. In Martin Buber's terms, it acts as the field of force between the "I" and the "Thou" in God. The original energy that is active in the breath of God and manifest in the history of creation is also the origin of the Son. This is expressed in the idea of the procreation of Jesus by the Holy Spirit and is purposefully emphasized in the creeds and confessions of the church.

This Trinitarian association of the revelation of Jesus Christ with the God of Israel was the basis for rejecting the gnosticism which was so attractive to many Christians in the first few centuries. It must have been very tempting for a downtrodden and impotent minority to see the repressive and violent world as ruled over by an evil god and thus to conceive of the God who revealed himself in Jesus Christ as the God of love who snatches his own people from a world doomed to extinction and leads them into eternal life. Indeed, this dualistic understanding of God and the world haunted Christianity like a shadow, and it is thus all the more important to remember that the early church's option for a

Trinitarian understanding of God meant a categorical rejection of dualistic belief.

The Albenga mosaic represents these ideas from a Christological perspective. The rule of the crucified Lord is portrayed cosmically, in accordance with Trinitarian theology. We acknowledge and believe in the ultimate Word of God when we recognize the Son's self-emptying "to the point of death — even death on a cross" (Phil. 2:8). Only in Jesus' death do we recognize who God really is. Only self-sacrificial love reveals what the creation in its ambivalence cannot bear out: that the vital principle of God's creative and preserving activity is nothing other than love. The nature of God's love is revealed only in the depths of *kenosis*. The cross illuminates the divine energy that was also vitally at work in the creation and in God's covenantal loyalty. If we conceive the Trinity from the basis of Christ himself, we may say that the *rûah* also proceeds from the Son, because by proceeding from the Son the *rûah* sheds light on the meaning and *telos* of creation and thus is recognized as the "power of love".[4]

Precisely because the cross and Christ's descent into hell represent the nadir of self-emptying and therefore the zenith of love, the resurrection and ascension are to be seen as the fulfilment of creation and thus the beginning of what Tillich calls the "new being".[5] The beginning and end of ages are contained, borne and assured in the tension between the Father and the Son in the power of the Holy Spirit. Precisely in God's Trinitarian form, God becomes a dynamic symbol of a power containing space and time. God encompasses the birth and death of every living thing. Not even a sparrow falls to the ground without his knowledge (Matt. 10:29ff.). God encompasses the rise and fall of nations and civilizations and the beginning and end of the life-cycles of this cosmos. "'I am the Alpha and the Omega,' says the Lord God, who is and who was and who is to come, the Almighty" (Rev. 1:8; cf. 21:6; 22:13).

In examining the first creation narrative of Genesis, we saw how Israel transformed its neighbours' static myths of origin into an historical myth of a God active in time. The exodus experiences with a God who intervenes with his liberating action and reveals an open covenantal history through messengers and prophets helped people to see the creation as part of the covenant rather than merely its "external basis" (Barth). This myth laid to rest the idea that the circumstances of life were decisively and immutably laid down and ordained "in the beginning", so that thereafter they could only be mimetically reproduced and represented in rites and festivals. The dynamic historical myth of Israel made it possible to combine the elements of contingency, conjunctures and new beginnings with the experiences of the rhythms of creation in a mutually explanatory way. The central symbol for this myth is YHWH, the tetragram commonly rendered as "Yahweh", essentially the formula for a God who indeed cannot and may not be named, determined or in any way limited by human definitions. "I am who I am" is the formula for a God who opens up history and is contingent, and whose inexplicability and futurity can only be borne in humility. For thousands of years Jewish belief has tried to speculate on the purposes and activity of this unnamable God — a process of "work" on the YHWH-myth that can only evoke respectful admiration.

With the revelation of Jesus of Nazareth as the crucified and resurrected Messiah, however, a fundamentally new situation arose, demanding the development of a new myth in response. Wherever Christ is acknowledged as God's ultimate Word, a new "unity" is established (to use Tillich's term). The revelation of the cross and resurrection, the eschatological aspect of the fulfilment of creation and the vision of a child-parent relationship with God extend and transform the myths of the creation and the covenant history of Israel. In the YHWH-myth the Hebrew Bible maintains a monist image of God, of which "Hear, O Israel: YHWH our God is one YHWH" (Deut. 6:4) is a prime example, and the *rûah* (*sophia, shekinah*) displays only that aspect apparent to the earth. The Christ-revelation, however, offers a Trinitarian image of God, one no longer characterized by unnamability but indeed by definability. This triune God is called Father, Mother, Son. Only because God is accessible in this way in the image of the Trinity can we conceive of God meaningfully as three "Persons", although this concept constantly risks falling into an anthropomorphism that limits the cosmic significance of the Christian image of God. Such an anthropocentric and personal restriction is impermissible precisely because love is a dimension of creation and the life-blood of all creatures.

Accordingly, Christian faith has developed an historical myth that is qualified both protologically and eschatologically. The symbol of creation testifies to the love that "was" since time immemorial. The symbol of the kingdom of God bears witness to the love that "comes" and thus places all life in the light of a prevenient grace. The symbol of eternal life testifies to a love that "is". In other words, the "project" of creation and the "project" of redemption come together and become one. They are realized in unison because they find their common basis in sacrificial love. We call this the *soul of the world*.

Only through the notion of *perichoresis* can this Trinitarian concept of God be adequately explicated. It permits us to envision the dynamic and intersubjective relations in God. When this concept is lost, we are bound to end up with monarchical, binitarian or monist images of God.[6]

Nevertheless, it is important to insist that this concept is fully realized only if it also refers to the "work" of this Trinitarian God. If, as a relational model of Trinitarian theology, it is limited to theology (in the strict sense of the doctrine of God), it remains abstract. Instead we must stress that the *history of creation and redemption* also has a perichoretic aspect. The salvation of the individual, the welfare of creatures and the peace of communities are interactive. The justification of an individual human being, the assurance of sanctification in the "community of saints" and healing care for the wounds of an endangered world permeate one another. But such a rift has constantly occurred in the history of Christianity, separating creation from the kingdom of God in the sense of a dualism of this world and the world beyond. That has led to a rift between heaven and earth, a separation of soul and body, a split between humanity and nature and a division between church and world, faith and eros, piety and science. We can counter all such forms of dualism only on the basis of a Trinitarian-perichoretic paradigm.

We may understand the history of church and theology as a ceaseless process of "work on the Christ-myth". At the same time, however, we have to concede that we now live in an era when the transforming power of this myth has faded. This is not the place to go into all the historical factors that have contributed to this — the influence of Arab civilization, the rediscovery of Greek philosophy, the Copernican revolution in the understanding of the universe, the discovery and conquest of new continents and the mastery of nature through new sciences and methods of production. The "project" of modernity is due to powerful new mythological images, including the Renaissance image of humanity and concept of power, with all the variations we know from the works and deeds of Michelangelo, Descartes, Francis Bacon, Machiavelli, Fernando Cortez and many others. We also recall in this context the particular mythology emanating from the Enlightenment and progressive thought in science, technology and economics, to say nothing of such vile examples as Alfred Rosenberg's Nazi *Myth of the Twentieth Century*.

The apocalyptic crisis of our own age is certainly also a crisis of these modern myths. But Christianity too has to face the question: Are we supported by the myth of the merciful God revealed in Christ? Or has its abuse through history discredited it to the point of unrecognizability? Do we perhaps live in an age that needs a new revelation?

We must not forget that many people believe just that. Many individuals who are open-minded and prepared for responsibility and commitment no longer expect anything more from the God of the Christians. While Christian theology may sound fine, in the end it turns out to be abstract and irrelevant. The churches seem far too conformist and imprisoned by their disputes and divisions to speak with one voice when challenged by the most threatening crises of our time.

The New Age movement is no doubt to be seen as a quest for a universal post-modern myth. In the course of this search, suppressed and esoteric traditions are receiving a new emphasis, along with philosophies and rites from other religions, especially the so-called nature-religions.

Is the Christian myth finished? Of course such a question is tantamount to a self-fulfilling prophecy, for if we say Yes, we contribute to its failure. If we say No, we are once again summoned to give "an accounting for the hope that is in us" (1 Pet. 3:15).

To avoid any misunderstanding, it is not a matter of asking whether there could or should be any single comprehensive myth for our threatened world. Here we must remember Tillich. A myth is not made but arises from the power of a new revelation. In any case, I am convinced that the present crisis is of such unprecedented gravity that all religions should consider themselves challenged to work on transforming their understanding of the world and the practice that comes out of it.

The ultimate danger we now face confronts Christianity with an alternative: dualism or Trinity, that is, division or unity of our life resources, betrayal or integration of creation. From the prayer to the Creator Spirit we drew the image of an absolutely faithful and yet powerful God — an image which only now, when we find ourselves on the edge of self-destruction, discloses its dynamic and integrative significance. It unites creation and redemption, heals the division between nature and humanity, joins the peace of nature with the peace of nations and links the welfare and rights of each individual with the well-being and justice of all creatures. It resists the chaos that menaces us on all sides. Thus it keeps faith with the cosmos.

This is the power that sustains heaven and earth and every-thing therein and fills them with life. This is the power that exerts its creative and constructive thrust in the history of the cosmos. Wherever this Holy Spirit opens our eyes, love is acknowledged to be the mystery of God, the mystery of life and the mystery of all salvation. Wherever the Spirit is the soul of the whole, Christ's cosmic radiation is apparent. Where God is all in all, everything receives new power and strength. The one who is Alpha and Omega speaks: "See, I am making all things new!" (Rev. 21:5).

NOTES

[1] I am indebted for this reference to Dr U. Arnold of the art archive and reference division of the North Elbian Evangelical Academy in Hamburg.

[2] *Systematic Theology*, Vol. I, Chicago, 1951, pp.91f. (italics added).

[3] H. Blumenberg, *Die Arbeit am Mythos*, Frankfurt am Main, 1979.

[4] On the *filioque* question see, among others, J. Moltmann, *The Spirit of Life*, esp. pp.306ff.

[5] For example, Latin American liberation theologian P. Trigo considers creation theology meaningful only as the development of the resurrection message. Cf. *Creación y Historia en el Proceso de Liberación*, Madrid and Sao Paulo, 1988; and "Creación y Mundo Material", in J. Ellacuria and J. Sobrino, *Mysterium Liberationis*, vol. II, Madrid, 1990.

[6] Cf J. Moltmann, *The Spirit of Life*, pp.289ff.

Part II
Creator Spirit
Soul of My Soul

Chapter 8

Soul of My Soul

In the first part of this book we looked at the Spirit of God as the "soul of the world", taking this as a typical mythological term for the fundamental power which ultimately sustains the cosmos and defends it from all threatening forces. Now we shall turn to this power as the "soul of my soul", for the energy at work in the greatest of all things is also effective in the smallest. This is perhaps more obvious in Hebrew than in English, for *rûah* is the life-producing energy that can grow into a hurricane, but can also calm down to the gentlest breeze, a scarcely perceptible breath that permeates all living things.

Since this power surges forth as God's essence, it is not in any way neutral. It is experienced as creative and fruitful love, as passionate self-sacrifice and as the power to resist everything destructive and meaningless.

The word "soul" reflects something of this wealth of meaning. It implies an omnipresent, loyal and loving power. When we speak of our soul, we try to express the quality which constitutes our vitality and personhood. The soul dwells in our body, but is not materially discernible in any particular organ. It permeates our consciousness, personality and overall temperament, yet is something more than reason or heart. The soul is the essence of our singularity and therefore is not something static, but something fluid that comes and goes, rather like breathing.

Nothing determines our subjective human being more emphatically than our soul; yet this soul does not turn the individual into a self-sufficient and isolated monad. On the contrary, the soul is the element of constant communication and exchange. When this exchange ceases, we are as good as dead. Hence what we call the "soul" is the unique power that makes every human an "open system". Just as we depend fundamentally on the air around us, so we are receptive to other influences. All our senses join us to the world that surrounds us. Our skin, which protects us, at the same time makes us permeable and constantly vulnerable. What presses in upon us can make us physically and mentally sick. When our psyche is disturbed and our soul in tumult, it is as if the very life of our body begins to atrophy, for the human body is the best picture of the human soul.

Receptivity and permeability are essential aspects not only of our biological life. They also constitute our special nature as historical and social beings. The soul is the core of our subjectivity. While this enables us to operate constructively in society, it also renders us sensitive, susceptible and vulnerable.

The unprecedented dangers and burdens of our time also have unparalleled effects on our soul. In the following chapters I shall try to show that these instances of global destructiveness manifest themselves much more comprehensively than is often admitted as afflictions of the human soul.

It is dangerously naive to assume that our soul's resources could remain unimpaired when social and ecological devastation is increasing everywhere. But while it is important to assess critically the economic, political and social factors that contribute to the misery of our world, it would be simple-minded to suppose that a mere change in these factors would end our spiritual misery.

Since there is a continuous interchange between outward circumstances and the forces of the human soul, social psychological considerations are closely related to economic, ecological and political factors. What used to be known as the "cure of souls" must become a basic factor in the analysis of our situation and a fundamental part of any alternative strategy. But this also means that we have to think constructively about pastoral care and overcome the mistrust of it that still prevails in many churches, especially in the third world. To be sure, much of this mistrust is warranted. Memories are far too fresh of pastoral practice that ignored the social, economic or political causes of the mental and spiritual agony of souls in distress, and thus could be experienced only as pious uplift or even another instrument of repression in the hands of the powerful. These forms of retreat from the world reflected and reinforced a dualist view of faith and the world, claiming to save the "soul" while leaving the world and history to their own devices. This is of course an illusion: no care for the world means no care for the soul.

The inordinate demand for therapy in industrial societies is itself a sign of mental disturbance, of distress of soul, and therefore must be taken most seriously. On the other hand, we must dispel the impression that there are no souls under stress in increasingly impoverished societies; indeed, such problems can be overlooked precisely because physical and social disorder is all too obvious there.

An ecumenical theology that faces up to the vast demands of our time must concentrate much more intensively on developing an *ecumenical pastoral care*. I understand this as work on behalf of the vital energy that ensouls and sustains not only humans but all creatures. Pastoral care is a deeply personal concern, for it centres on the core of our subjective nature. But it is also profoundly social and public, because it has to do with the conditions of receptivity and therefore of growth among and between forms of life. The unprecedented burdens of our age require that we enlarge and strengthen not only the ability of our souls to bear burdens, but also their capacity for experience. This is possible only if we take effective account of that power which holds creation together and thus can also enable our souls to soar beyond their present restrictions.

Chapter 9

Global Threats and Psychic Numbing

The psychological dilemma

Millions of years of evolution have taught human consciousness to react to the most varied dangers. Our senses help us to cope almost instinctively with direct physical threats. They are the instruments of the animal fear that has ensured our survival since amphibian times. Of course, there is a proverb which says that anxiety is our worst counsellor, but the fear I am referring to here comprises the natural tension and attentiveness that control our behaviour in menacing situations.

Alongside this basic biological equipment for reacting appropriately to dangers, communal devices to ensure survival have developed in the course of human socialization. Family, clan, kin, lineage and nation have these defensive functions. One could in fact portray the history of civilization as a history of constantly extending and refining defence-mechanisms. The grandiose intentions of the Great Wall of China, designed to protect the Middle Kingdom against incursions from the north, may seem incredible to us today, yet the Wall would seem to have fulfilled this function for many years. It was a powerful achievement of social defence. The dikes on the North Sea coast of the Netherlands and Germany, built to protect the land and its inhabitants from storm-tides, are no less impressive. Modern societies possess increasingly complex security systems: health care, sewage removal, pension and social security schemes, traffic-control systems and so on.

All these are responses to dangers to life and limb that we can directly discern, for our personal and collective experience tells us how threatening enemy attacks, floods, epidemics and social impoverishment are. These often very complicated social mechanisms for regulating and limiting danger depend on our inherited danger sensors, our senses. But now consider the dangers that have piled up over the last fifty years. Our senses are useless when we remember the radioactivity released at Chernobyl, for exam-

ple. We neither smell nor taste this danger; we do not see or hear
or feel it. Our inherited fear-sensors are not designed to recognize
this threat.

The case of nuclear weapons is similar. For obvious reasons,
they are usually concealed from us. But when we do see them,
their phallic immensity may elicit a certain reluctant admiration —
from men, at least — more readily than a sense of their menace.
Our instincts and sensibilities simply cannot comprehend that
these devices can destroy hundreds of thousands of people and
devastate all forms of life in a few minutes. We know from
experience, and our senses also tell us, the meaning of an invasion
by soldiers and tanks, and even of an onslaught of poison-gas
rockets. But the implications of an attack by nuclear missiles are
beyond our understanding.

It is the same with ecological dangers. Our senses do not
enable us to perceive the destruction of the ozone layer. It does
not affect, indeed touch, us directly. Doctors may be aware of the
connection between the ozone layer and skin cancer, but most
people are sensibly impervious to this causal association. Further-
more, the time lapse between ultraviolet radiation and car-
cinogenic reactions contributes to our insensitivity to the destruction of the ozone layer.

The case of the smog above our cities or of the dying fish in the
rivers that flow through them is different, because here our senses
can see the evidence. So we react with alarm. But again we
encounter the difficulty that is raised by nuclear weapons and the
diminishing ozone layer: how are we to defend ourselves? These
dangers are far too complex for the acquired array of social
defence-mechanisms. Their global spread makes legal and control
systems devised within national boundaries antiquated and ineffective.

When we consider the impoverishment of entire regions of the
world, other aspects come into play. Think only of the physical
distance involved. What happens in far-off parts of the globe does
not affect us directly. It is not *our* children who are starving. The
masses of hungry people belong to another world, as the very
term "third world" suggests.

This is said without moral indignation. Of course there is such
a thing as social solidarity, and what we call altruism. But that too
is a major strategy for minimizing danger, usually limited along
the lines of boundaries of kin, race or country. This is also the

case within the so-called third world. People in Central America have a very vague conception of people in Africa and cannot imagine that the poverty there could be just as bad as their own.

At one time third-world support groups protesting the appalling wages of coffee plantation workers used the slogan: "There's blood in this coffee". We can easily see why this slogan was ineffective. The connection between coffee and blood is both theatrical and unsavoury. It evokes an instinctively defensive response. Moreover, the distance between the concerns of the workers in coffee plantations and breakfast tables in Europe or North America is so great as to be scarcely conducive to empathy and solidarity on our part.

None of this is really changed by the fact that electronic communications media sometimes bring the ghastly poverty of workers in distant lands into our own living rooms. The more we learn about it, the less we want to hear about it. The more data we receive about it, the greater our sense of confusion and overkill. As it hits the borders of our imagination the flood of information evokes our instinctively defensive reactions.

Besides being too difficult to feel, too invisible, too distant and too complex, there is another factor that makes the dangers of our time unprecedented: their *futurity*. Our existing danger sensors react to actual, present dangers and to those that return with a certain degree of probability. The danger of Chernobyl, however, is not only the number of deaths and evacuations it caused directly, but the damage that has already been caused and is not yet apparent. The fire in the nuclear reactor cores spread its ashes over the future — by means of genetic damage and poisoning of the soil, the food chain and ground-water. Our fear-mechanisms are powerless against this kind of danger. We cannot lament tomorrow's dead. And Chernobyl is only one example. This destruction of the future would reach its absolute form in the kind of nuclear winter that would necessarily follow an atomic war.

The impoverishment of societies over vast regions of the world has this same tendency to extend beyond its present-day effects. It is no one-off catastrophe, from which a society could recover, that forty thousand children under five die every day from largely avoidable diseases that are due to or affected by hunger. It is the result of a process of impoverishment that spans the generations and has already reached out into the future. The children of today who survive in need and poverty will tomorrow bring into the world even more children who will surely die of hunger. This systemic impoverishment is no time-bomb ticking away but a bomb that has already exploded. It has exploded into the future, making its crater in tomorrow's world as well as today's.

The same is true of the destruction of the rain-forests. The bomb of climatic disasters has probably already exploded, even though its havoc will become manifest only around 2030.

The foregoing may suffice as an outline of the psychological dilemma of our time. Human instincts and feelings cannot adequately respond to the unparalleled dangers, although a response is absolutely necessary for the sake of the future of life. By definition the unprecedented has no place in the make-up of the experiences and instincts which largely determine our behaviour. We can approach it only through simulation models and computer-assisted scenarios. Our reason and imagination have the power to conceive of and portray phenomena that have never before existed. Then on the basis of the global analyses thus obtained, we can formulate appeals for a new global moral effort. The more complex and probable these analyses become, the more urgent and unremitting the moral demands.

But why do they not achieve the necessary effects? Because the co-operation of the soul is missing. Because our instincts react too slowly. Because our counsellor fear has not taken the measure of the times.

Our psychological dilemma is that the dangers by which we are threatened have overtaken us too rapidly. Having taken by surprise certain faculties of our soul — our psychological abilities to adapt and respond — they have incapacitated them. We are literally incapable, psychologically speaking, of grasping the danger.

Psychic numbing

Experiencing the unprecedented inevitably has a dislocating effect on the psyche. No one has seen this more clearly than the US psychologist Robert Jay Lifton. He uses the term "numbing" to describe the peculiar "ability" of the human psyche to keep on existing under conditions of "death immersion". Lifton encountered this phenomenon in his studies on survivors of Hiroshima.[1] They helped him to see that the "killing of feelings" can become a way of survival under extreme threats. The only way not to lose one's mind is to make it insensitive to the onslaught of painful images, to reduce the range of feeling, to go numb.

Numbing is the protective mode not only of victims under extreme stress but also of victimizers. In his book *The Nazi Doctors*[2] Lifton has shown that medical professionals who worked in Nazi concentration camps during the second world war numbed all feelings of remorse and responsibility for their victims. Even thirty years later, when Lifton undertook to interview them, they remained insensitive to any feelings of grief or repentance about what they had done.

Lifton maintains that numbing occurs not only in these extreme situations but that it is in fact a very widespread phenomenon.[3] One might even say that in the degree to which we become aware of the unprecedented threats of our age, we are prone to react with various forms of numbing.

How does numbing manifest itself in our everyday lives? What kind of pathological reactions can be detected? In the three chapters that follow, I shall concentrate on three types of numbing which are significant in today's world: cynicism, fundamentalism and violentism.

NOTES

[1] *Death in Life: Survivors of Hiroshima*, New York, 1st ed., 1968.
[2] Subtitled *Medical Killing and the Psychology of Genocide*, New York, 1986.
[3] Cf. his books *The Life of the Self*, New York, 1976; *The Broken Connection*, New York, 1983; and (with Richard Falk) *Indefensible Weapons*, New York, 1982.

Chapter 10

Cynicism:
The Desperation of the Powerful

One of the pathological social manifestations of numbing is cynicism. I am not referring here to the sort of sardonic remark sometimes known as "black humour", which may even liberate us from cynicism proper. I am concerned here with cynicism as an habitual perversion of how reality is perceived. Such cynicism is most characteristic of professions that come into active contact with the global threats of our age. It is particularly evident among journalists, business and industrial managers, politicians and members of the various branches of the military and secret services.

Numbing from too much information
Every day journalists are bombarded with thousands of news items from all over the world. Many of these stories are so cruel and shocking that they cannot be dealt with sympathetically. Day after day thousands of news items vanish into the wastepaper basket — and with them disappear the stories of the destinies, sufferings and hopes of innumerable people.

Journalists have no choice but to make a selection from the flood of news. They must take into account the views and political preferences of publishers, editors and broadcasting committees. Cost and competition are further considerations. In one sense, "bad news is good news" for journalists, but at the same time it must not be *too* depressing. So information and entertainment have to be mixed judiciously (the US media have even coined the arch-cynical term "info-tainment").

This daily pressure leads inevitably to a throwaway attitude to the truth. My point here is not to accuse individual journalists of moral culpability, but to observe that they work in a setting whose very structure is cynical. This is conducive to a purely technical treatment of human happiness and unhappiness, suffering and disasters. Personal concern and empathy are impossible to maintain.

Cynicism comprises both the pretence of truth and the transformation of truth into entertainment. As consumers of the media, we too share in this cynicism and are infected by it. We consume news as we do publicity. We are not meant to see how the relation of news to truth is manipulated. On Costa Rican television, for instance, advertising is inserted almost seamlessly into the newscasts. In the USA, when no live film material is available to illustrate a televised news story, it may be simulated in the studio without any clear indication that this is happening. Cynicism makes the communication of truth a form of entertainment which turns viewers into voyeurs.

Numbing from too much money

Industrial managers also work in a structurally cynical environment. When one automobile manufacturer in 1990 advertised a new twelve-cylinder model as "environmentally friendly", this may have been true in comparison with other twelve-cylinder cars. But the claim was arch-cynical, because it suggested that running a twelve-cylinder internal combustion engine could actually *help* the environment.

Managers and industrialists are much better aware than others of the ecological and medical risks of their products. They read the scientific evaluations of their own research laboratories. They know that a product forbidden in a European country because it contains environmentally dangerous substances will also damage the environment in Peru or Thailand, even though its manufacture there is not yet outlawed — or the laws can be circumvented by bribery. It is profoundly cynical of Italian refrigerator manufacturers to move their factories to China in order to reduce the level of chlorofluorocarbon (CFC) emissions at home. Any manager is intelligent enough to know that this is sheer hypocrisy: after all, the earth has only one ozone layer. But industrialists allow themselves to be dictated to not only by increased production targets, profit goals and fear of losing market shares to the competition, but also by concern for any erosion of their personal prestige.

Here again my point is not to level a moral charge of cynicism against business people but to observe that a conflict with ecology is built into the very structure of contemporary economies. Anyone who claims to be able, in the setting and under the pressures of the market economy, to do something fundamental to enhance the vitality of our earth's ecosystems is deluding himself or herself and us. Even the most effective catalytic converter for a twelve-cylinder automobile is merely ecological cosmetics, and a cynical advertising gimmick.

Structural cynicism results from massive denial of the ethical contradictions in a world economy that devotes ever more resources to constantly more extravagant consumption by an ever smaller section of the world's population. It thus condemns an increasingly greater part of humankind and ever larger expanses of nature to increasingly less curable impoverishment.

Numbing from too much power

Political misuse of power is another area of cynicism. In 1978 a former high-ranking officer with thirteen years' service in the US Central Intelligence Agency wrote a vivid description of how law and justice were systematically abused for the sake of a major power's interests.[1] The CIA's destabilization campaigns and corruption programmes — whether in Vietnam, Angola, Guatemala, Panama or El Salvador — exhibit the same pattern. Hiding behind the political and military superiority of the USA, and protected by the apathy of a public used to political scandals, this secret service penetrates sovereign states and tries to destroy them from within.

Evidence is growing that in European countries also secret service organizations have begun to form covert paramilitary groups and terror units, which operate like criminal gangs. And since the end of the 1980s, the breakdown of communism in Eastern and Central Europe has disclosed the cynicism with which the old power cliques operated and spied on their own people.

The cynical use of power produces "grey zones" in which justice can no longer rule because there is no legal authority to exert control.

Such cynicism, rooted in systemic contempt for the norms of international law, undermines the sovereignty of states and their legislation. It tears great holes in the fragile fabric of legal structures within and between countries. Pressures, threats, intimidation, extortion and torture corrupt the social networks on whose reliability all life in community depends.

This kind of misuse of power by secret services also does profound harm to the fabric of the community of nations. It expresses an habituation to power that considers itself free from law, justice and the duty of protecting the weak. Thus justice as the attempt of human beings to live and deal with one another in peace and concord becomes a mockery.

A premonition of chaos

Our interest here is with cynicism as a symptom of "numbing", not with an ethical discussion of its criminal aspects. Of course it is clear that there are additional criminal abuses of power within the vacuum of justice produced by secret services. Of all the manifestations of cynicism in association with power, torture is certainly the most outrageous. Of course there are managers who personally choose further to pervert the cynicism built into the market economy, for example, by exporting weapons to war-prone areas. Of course there are media people who go even further in perverting the cynicism built into news-gathering.

At the same time, many people in the vocations I have chosen here as examples are well aware of the inherent cynicism of their professions. Without such people the quest for new ethical standards for the media, the economy and politics would be inconceivable. In this context, however, I am dealing with cynicism as a socially manifested form of psychic numbing that is rooted in a system, not in individuals. It is a widespread phenomenon, especially in so-called centres of power. Such cynicism is not a problem of poor people but of rich people. It does not beset people who lack power but those who have too much power.

In fact, we might call cynicism a perversion of power. The media, the economy and the secret services show that a cynical reaction is almost inevitable when there is excessive news, money and power. A permanent confrontation with ethical dilemmas leads to apathy and indifference, whereas power seems desirable. This tension is unbearable in the long run, because very few people ever manage to break absolutely with power. Most people continue in a pathologically numbed way of dealing with the ethical implications of their power and try to hide their despair in cynical mockery.

"For what will it profit you if you gain the whole world but forfeit your life? Or what will you give in return for your life?" (Matt. 16:26). The force of Jesus' questions remains. If you lose your soul, that is, if you become dead in a living body, the world is also dead to you. Whatever you gain cannot restore the lost vitality of the soul.

Cynicism knows only today and the pleasure of immediate gratification. It has lost interest in the well-being of the whole. It no longer cares about the right of the weak, or the weaker part of creation, least of all about the rights of the future. It has ceased to believe that life still has a tomorrow. Cynicism is an attack on the Spirit of God, who is the power of the future. The motto of cynicism is *"après moi le déluge"*. It is thus a premonition of chaos.

NOTE

[1] John Stockwell, *In Search of Enemies*, New York, 1978.

Chapter 11

Fundamentalism:
The Desperation of the Powerless

No one can live without certain fundamentals. The house of our life needs supporting walls and pillars if it is to stand. The most important of these basic supports include not only the love of our parents, the care and nurture of our family and the familiar surroundings of our village or neighbourhood, but also the norms and values of our culture, the traditions of our people and the great rhythms of nature.

But the house of life in which we live, although it rests on such fundamental supports, is not identical to them. What my life is derived from does not determine where it takes me. My life proves its worth precisely in my own use of my origins, becoming ready and open for what is to come by transforming what has been. This applies to each individual life and to the lives of nations. Customs, culture, even religion are manifestations of this process of appropriation, transformation and self-development. This certainly includes a degree of political and economic freedom as well as an obvious confidence about the openness and trust-worthiness of life and the prospects of a life beyond one's own death.

But what happens to this essential process of appropriation and transformation if the freedom and space for development are radically restricted? What happens if trust in the future vanishes in a long night of impoverishment and degradation, homeless-ness and disillusionment? Then creative encounter with the fundamentals of culture and politics is replaced by fundamental-ist projects.

Fundamentalism as despair at excessive need

It is not surprising that the message of fundamentalist groups receives an enthusiastic welcome precisely in those parts of the third world where not only economic poverty but cultural and political impoverishment are widespread. I shall cite only two examples.

1. *Evangelical sects in Central America.* Evangelical and Pentecostal churches are mushrooming in every country of Central America. *Templos* and *iglesias* where people, many of them women, assemble almost every evening are found in the poor quarters of cities, in disintegrating neighbourhoods and in villages where social destabilization has taken hold.

Some observers attribute this phenomenon to the covert operations of the US Central Intelligence Agency and the zealous activities of fundamentalist missionaries from North America. To be sure, the CIA is somewhat involved, and the influence of the "Electronic Church" from the USA is discernible, amplified by the often massive economic resources available to these evangelical groups. But the exceedingly rapid implantation of this movement has more to do with the internal state of Central American societies. Religious fundamentalism in Central America is an indigenous religious manifestation that answers the profound needs of many people.

The evening service is an escape from the vileness of the *barrio*, a cherished refuge for people, especially women, who see their world as devoid of prospects. Here they listen to something that gives them meaning. Here a new community is available for those who have been driven from their land or dispossessed of the support of their rural or small-town way of life and for those in whose shacks television sets flicker with confusing images of a life they will never enjoy. The disturbing reality is one of a culture of poverty and the collapse of reliable worlds. Amidst all that, the community in the little *iglesia* is endowed with a protective, stabilizing significance. Here everyone is important. Here they shape together a community and liturgical life, whereas in the established churches the sacraments are merely "administered" to them and, as fits their social and economic status, they are virtually disenfranchised.

For such people it is obviously a godsend when preachers proclaim a God who loves a poor person such as I and wants to lead me into his paradise. It is liberating to hear that the world is full of suffering, injustice and death because it is ruled over by the devil, and cannot help me. No party or revolution can change the poverty of my life. How can anyone who belongs to the world of transience and death bring me life? Indeed, there can be no real life before death. It is immeasurably consoling to be told that I must wander here like a stranger in a dark vale of tears until God receives me into eternal life and wipes the tears from my eyes.

The attractiveness of this message lies in its bestowal of dignity on those deprived of it, in its simple presentation of a complicated world, but also in its contempt for the world as the human home and its concentration on a heaven located absolutely in the afterlife. Valuation of the individual means empowerment. The simplistic interpretation of the world tranquillizes the troubled heart. Hope in the world beyond makes suffering bearable. Disdain for social and political action takes away any responsibility for this "evil world".

2. *Arab and Islamic fundamentalism.* The Islamic Arab nations of the Middle East and North Africa remember the illustrious times of the warriors of Allah, when the Arab empire represented the very heights of science and scholarship, civilization and refinement, and the barbarian nations of Europe envied Arab achievements.

The longing for political power, which in the Arab world includes the religious strength of the Islamic faith, has become a nagging pain in centres where the decline from former greatness and subjection to European colonialism have been most obvious. In recent decades further humiliation has increased this anguish — not only military reversals at the hands of Israel but also the alienating effects of the behaviour and business practices of "unbelievers" and the immense changes and upheavals brought about by their modern technology.

Islamic fundamentalism is an immensely attractive alternative. A strict return to the virtues of the Prophet and a rigorous demonization of everything Western allow the profoundly disturbed and wounded individual a feeling of dignity, definition and purpose. This has created a fanatical following for politicians making messianic claims against the Western powers. Does dying matter if life has become so shameful and death opens up the road to paradise?

These two examples show that it is possible to speak of a *fundamentalism of the poor*. In these instances (which might be multiplied), fundamentalism is obviously the pathological consequence of a profound disorder that results from the absolute frustrations of cultural, political and religious impoverishment. This is fundamentalism arising from too much powerlessness.

Fundamentalism as despair at excessive complexity

Nevertheless it would be incorrect to imagine that fundamentalism arises only in situations of impoverishment. It also exists in rich Northern countries, not just among the underclass but in all sectors of the population and in major institutions. In such cases the stress of life results not so much from the experience of material, cultural and political impoverishment as from complex conditions that seem to have developed to the point where they are intolerable. Again, I shall cite only two examples.

1. *Vatican fundamentalism.* A salient example of this tendency is Roman Catholicism as represented by Pope John Paul II, the curia and a great number of bishops. Clearly the universal Catholic Church is in an extremely complex situation. If it is to respond realistically to people in their widely varied states of life, it has to reinterpret faith in new and imaginative ways.

Decisively and courageously, the Second Vatican Council set itself precisely this task. The resulting process of appropriation and transformation was taken further in some parts of the world, for example, by the Latin American bishops at Medellín (1968) and Puebla (1983). Sometimes this process has taken an even more radical form in the religious orders. The effects on the priesthood became unpredictable. The resulting situation is so complex that it has awakened deep anxieties not only in many parishes but above all among the bishops and in the Vatican itself. Was the whole institutional church facing collapse?

This life-crisis necessarily surfaced in its most pointed form in the crisis of the magisterium, the teaching office, and the priesthood, which together form the central support of the Catholic Church. On the one hand, there is a great shortage of priests, not least because many men can no longer sincerely lead a celibate life. On the other hand, women, more and more of whom are aware of a calling to the priesthood, are not allowed to be ordained.

The reaction of the Vatican and the episcopate to this complex yet far from irresoluble situation has essentially been a fundamentalistic one. The opportunity to rethink the priestly office in the face of this complexity is passed by, and the rule of celibacy is more strictly enforced. Refusing women the priesthood creates even more disappointment and suffering. The consensus of doctrine and faith regarding questions of sexual morality and family planning is interpreted restrictively despite its unhappy consequences for population policy and its effects on the faithful. These are but a few aspects of a petrification that has taken hold of the see of St Peter and the central institutions of the Catholic Church.

2. *Political fundamentalism.* Fundamentalism "from above" exists not only in a religious form, and not only in the mixture of orthodoxy and politics characteristic of Islam. During the 1980s, for example, the US administration of Ronald Reagan was essentially fundamentalist. "Reaganomics" was a simplistic reduction of the complexity of US society in the areas of social and economic policy. This led to a diminution of social initiatives by the state and to a growing polarization between the rich and increasingly impoverished sectors of the population. While some sectors of US society benefited from increasing plenty, others were sinking to levels reminiscent of the third world.

President Reagan's foreign policy was also characterized by a dualist notion of the world, sometimes quite reminiscent of evangelical apocalyptic. This friends-and-foes vision of things skewed any appropriate approach to the global political situation. For many years it was the East-West antagonism which legitimized this approach. When Mikhail Gorbachev's break with the fundamentalist rigidity of Soviet Marxism-Leninism destroyed that particular dualism, the dichotomy was transferred to the opposition between North and South.

It may seem paradoxical, but this kind of fundamentalism of the powerful is basically an expression of the experience of powerlessness. The complexity of world society can no longer be mastered by traditional political means. The experience of impotence resulting from the inability to master and control the world leads to a fundamentalist and reactionary misuse of power.

Apocalyptic fundamentalism

Behind the fundamentalism of the poor and the fundamentalism of the powerful we find another mode, which we may call *apocalyptic*. This also results from a perception of the increasingly complex and chaotic state of the world. These global dangers are integrated into a dualistic picture of history which emphasizes the last days and an ultimate apocalyptic struggle. With the biblical literalism characteristic of classical Protestant fundamentalism, apocalyptic writings such as the book of Daniel are combined with the book of Revelation to be interpreted as prophesying an imminent collapse of our world. The protagonists are Christ and the antichrist. The nations and great powers are secondary actors who, with all their destructive potential, unconsciously and involuntarily act out the Almighty's ultimate historical plan. The final battle laying waste the earth is concentrated on Armageddon. Ultimately, the sinful powers of the world will destroy themselves and Christ will create a new heaven and a new earth.

This kind of apocalyptic fundamentalism can hardly be dismissed as a bizarre and peripheral phenomenon. These fantasies appeal to the profound and widespread anxieties of many people regarding a future whose dark promise offers only danger and chaos. They betray a mute despair at the powerlessness of people of good will, a desperation that has decided that this world is irredeemable. The only course is to flee it. Desperation over the world's complexities is transformed into hatred of this "evil world".

Apocalyptic fundamentalism is thus the opposite of that process of appropriating and transforming what has been handed down which gives life to every culture and religion. It no longer worries about combatting poverty, avoiding wars or promoting the harmony of ecosystems so as to encourage justice, peace, security, harmony and joy here on earth and to honour the Creator by service to the creation. Indeed, it scornfully dismisses this basic duty of humankind as "world-improvement" and even disobedience to God. There is no further trace of any inward connection between God and creation or faith and practice. There is only the ultimate and now absolute rift between a transgalactic Creator and believing souls freed from their sinful nature on the one side and the cohorts of the damned on the other. The dualism we have come to know as the fundamental structure of sin becomes the constitutive structure of a certain conception of salvation. A quietistic bleakness of heart replaces passionate and tender empathy. Faith and hope are now associated with uncharitableness. Thus the apocalyptic obsession with the death of the universe is shown to be a straightforward perversion of Christian hope.

All types of fundamentalist systems depend on an absolute dualism. Their reaction to the seemingly insoluble burden and complexity of the world is a series of essentially violent and radical simplifications which evoke violent conflicts. Fundamentalist systems cannot understand the trinitarian nature of God and thus of creation. They are widespread expressions of a disordered capacity for religious experience. This inability to trust is ultimately a betrayal of God's Spirit, the soul of the world.

Chapter 12

Violentism:
Turning the World Back to Chaos

What happens when human beings are exposed to too much violence — not only for a short moment but over a prolonged period of time or even continuously? Surely situations of "violence immersion", to adapt an expression of Lifton's, must have an intensely disorienting impact on our psychic constitution. As an alternative to madness or suicide, it seems to me, one way that people learn to live with violence is by beginning to love it. This libidinous identification with violence is an extreme state of numbing which we might call "violentism".

Two examples may elucidate this observation. One is evident in the methods used to train death squads, such as the notorious *Caibiles* in Guatemala. The object of these methods is to create in the trainees a virtually erotic attachment to their weapons, while at the same time deliberately destroying all the links they have with their home communities. The destruction of this continuity goes hand in hand with the creation of self-hate and of an attraction to means of destruction in which the instruments of killing become objects of desire.

A second case has been observed among research and construction teams in factories where nuclear bombs are made. These people are constantly faced with the fact that they are producing instruments of extreme annihilative power. What often happens is that they begin to "love the Bomb" — which oddly corresponds to the phallic shape of missiles and nuclear weapons, though it would be too narrow to describe this attachment to instruments of extreme violence only in sexual terms. Lifton remarks that this fascination borders on the religious; after all, the Bomb is capable of doing what was hitherto reserved to God, namely to destroy the world.[1] This observation leads Lifton to conclude that "nuclearism... is the ultimate form of fundamentalism of our time".[2] We may add that nuclearism is a clear manifestation of violentism.

Of course, violence immersion is by no means confined to the two groups mentioned here. But these examples can help us to understand why and how violentism takes hold of people's lives. On the one hand is the constant exposure to extremely violent situations which seem only to offer two alternatives: complete negation (which would result in one or another form of self-destruction) or complete identification (which must result in the denial of such vital feelings as respect, shame and guilt). This exposure is accompanied by the experience of isolation. The bonds with home communities have been destroyed, only to be replaced by a group identity that is composed of self-hatred and violence.

On the other hand, the temporal element is extremely important. Life under the permanent presence of annihilation and death lacks any sense of continuity. Moreover, the "work" of such groups, that is, the promotion of death, is not in the service of the continuity of life but in making certain that life can be terminated at any moment. So violence becomes an object of libidinous fascination not in spite of its "deathfulness" but precisely *because* of it. It is the absence of continuity, the loss of a future, which must be seen as the central component of violentism.

We could also say that violentism expresses the apocalyptic horror that overwhelms us whenever the future appears to be swallowed up by death. When there is nothing to look forward to, when in fact all we do is to make certain that this nothingness is growing, then we are beset by a deep sense of confusion, frustration and anger, for which we compensate in lust for violence. This has become a widespread phenomenon in contemporary societies. Violentism is expressed not only in literature and movies of a pornographic nature; it has become a central theme of the mass-market "horror" novels on sale at any airport bookshop and of the "horror" films shown at mainstream cinemas in every city and town. The books of Stephen King come to mind here, but also David Lynch's film *Wild at Heart* or Oliver Stone's *Natural Born Killers*, to cite only a few examples.

Why do books and films of this sort attract so many millions of "ordinary" readers and viewers — women and men? I think we can only conclude that a profound relationship exists between the violence which they express and the feeling of senselessness and horror that has permeated our societies. After all, who knows whether we are not already trapped in ecological disasters? Who can guarantee that we will be protected from lunatics willing to unleash a nuclear holocaust?

In former times one's individual life was threatened from all sides, but time itself, that powerful stream of new possibilities coming to us from the future, remained certain. Although one's own life might soon be over, people were sure that life itself would go on. This confidence in life and time provided a deep sense of continuity and security and, not least, gave people a sense of direction, purpose and, therefore, morality.

However, when the future is already *passé*, the horror of the abysmal void creeps up from beneath all the foundations of life. When the future is denied, time plays havoc with us. And this is violence in its deepest form. So violentism is an expression of profound despair, because it seems as if the world is turning back to chaos.

NOTES

[1] *The Future of Immortality and Other Essays for a Nuclear Age*, New York, 1987, p.25.
[2] *Indefensible Weapons* (with R. Falk), p.95.

Chapter 13

In Search of a Spiritual Paradigm

The realities of too much power, too much misery and too much violence are characteristics of the unprecedented crisis in which humankind finds itself at the end of the modern era. Consequently, various forms of "numbing" have spread around the globe in epidemic proportions. In the preceding chapters we have looked at three of them: cynicism, fundamentalism and "violentism". How are we to understand these expressions of psychic dislocation in spiritual terms? Traditional theological concepts seem to be of little help.

If we were to draw on the mediaeval concept of "sin", we might describe "numbing" in terms of the deadly sin of *acedia*, that is, inertia. Inertia is a laziness of heart that springs from apathy. It is the inability — and not just the unwillingness — to feel the pathos, the suffering and pain, of a world out of joint. To be sure, it is possible to survive with a reduced and constricted sensitivity, but the price to be paid is a profound loss of intensity of feeling, creativity and vitality, in brief a restricted self. Human beings who have shrunk themselves with apathy suffer from a lack of compassion and grace; and that makes them inhuman, at times even monstrous. Inertia and apathy become part of a vicious circle as they in turn intensify and deepen cynicism, violence and destructiveness.

In the mythic language of the Christian faith, this could be called "lack of spirit", not merely in personal but in cosmic terms. Chaos, the perennial shadow of creation, is looming large on the horizon. So when we pray, "Come, Creator Spirit", we do so in the face of a struggle of cosmic proportions. It is a struggle that we address not only to redeem our numbed souls but to make room for the restoration of life on earth. This is a cry that comes *de profundis*, from the depths of a world engulfed by apocalyptic horrors, a cry that hopes for creation to keep on working.

The prayer for the Spirit also creates the space in which we are reminded of how the early Christian communities experienced the vitality and life-giving power of the *pneuma*. So as we look for a spiritual paradigm to cope with the destructive demons of our time, we want to learn from what our mothers and fathers of the faith in New Testament times had to say about how the breath of God went through their lives.

As I have said earlier, praying is a distinctly mythic mode of searching for alternatives and making room for images of new possibilities. Prayer has a lot to do with imagination. This leads me back to Robert J. Lifton. Although he claims no adherence to the Jewish or Christian faiths, he does in fact suggest processes of healing that have close similarities with the therapeutic impact of our faith.

Since Lifton is a psychologist, that which we have called "myth-work" appears in his books in psychological terms. He puts great emphasis on the specific human capacity of imagination and symbolization. "We live on images. As human beings we know our bodies and our minds only through what we can imagine. To grasp our humanity we need to structure these images into metaphors and models. Writers, artists and visionaries have always known this." With these programmatic sentences Lifton begins *The Broken Connection*, the book in which he presents his basic psychological paradigm in the most definitive manner.[1] Imagination, a central category, is the ongoing process of grounding and anticipating; it is the manner in which we humans connect our existence to our history and, beyond that, to our biology, that is, to the history of the universe.

This capacity is intimately linked to the continuity of collective life — also a central concept for Lifton, which can easily be paralleled to the mythic term "eternal life". This is the solid ground on which we manage our immediate problems and which enables us to connect the particular project of our life with all other life that has gone on before us and ever shall be.

The disturbing experience of our age is that this natural and instinctive connection has broken down. The basic trust in the continuity of collective life is shattered. In order to restore the life-sustaining processes of imagination, human beings need to cultivate their awareness. In Lifton's terms,

> awareness... includes the ability to anticipate and realize danger on the one hand and the capacity for knowledge and transcendental feeling on the other... Our present difficulty is that we must extend that imaginative access to include massive death and the possibility of total annihilation.[2]

Lifton's category of "awareness" includes three elements: anxiety, comfort and advocacy. *Anxiety* is closely related to the "art" of imagining threats of various kinds, including massive death.[3] In order for this anxiety to remain responsive and resilient, we need *comfort*, that is, the experience of centring which we get in loving relationships and caring communities.[4] Finally, our imaginative powers need to be expressed in clear and exemplary actions. This is where concrete acts of *advocacy* come into play.[5]

Lifton's paradigm provokes the theologian to seek a spiritual approach that would also attempt to reinforce the necessary processes of connecting and symbolizing. Obviously, the emphasis on community has a central role to play here. It is not enough to understand "community" only in human or even narrowly ecclesiastical terms. The reference to creation is constitutive in order to give due expression to the essential grounding of the psychic energies of human beings in the evolution of life. It seems to me that the neglect of this dimension in traditional concepts of pastoral care — and of psychology as a whole — has deprived it of its cosmological-communal anchorage.[6]

Moreover, it is clear that the element of comfort needs to be reasserted in light of the Christian tradition. The love of God is the fundamental witness of the Bible and provides the solid ground on which all life rests. Thus *solidarity* becomes a central category. The preferred term in the tradition of the Christian churches, "consolation", has over the centuries unfortunately lost a great deal of its original power.

Would anxiety be an adequate concept for a spiritual paradigm? Although Lifton's emphasis on enlightened and resolute anxiety appears realistic, I would maintain that it would be more in line with the biblical record to focus on the notion of *truth*.

Finally, Lifton's insistence on advocacy needs to be kept in mind because any spiritual paradigm that lacked practical and sustained commitment would be useless. Yet the idea of advocacy does not seem to me to be wholly appropriate. In Christian circles great attention has sometimes been given to the notion of "stewardship", but the shortcoming of this concept is that it tends to underscore the special role and place of the human over and above the rest of creation. In order to emphasize the dimension of continuity and steadfast care, I would prefer to focus on *endurance*.

Accordingly, in the following chapters I shall use the terms of truth, solidarity and endurance for a paradigm of ecumenical pastoral care. We shall look closely at each of these concepts in terms of its biblical reference and seek to elucidate its implications in the circumstances of contemporary life. I hope to show that the interdependence of these three notions can give substance and resilience to a paradigm that is seriously grounded in the awareness with which the *pneuma* is at work in our history.

NOTES

[1] Subtitled *On Death and the Continuity of Life*. This quotation is from p.3.

[2] *Ibid.*, p.392.

[3] *Ibid.*, p.125; cf. his references to Freud on *Angst*, pp.127ff.

[4] *Ibid.*, pp.121ff.

[5] *The Future of Immortality*, pp.277ff.; cf. his chapter on "Advocacy: The Person in the Paradigm", in *The Life of the Self*, pp.151-71.

[6] For a lucid elaboration of this see T. Roszak, *The Voice of the Earth*, New York, 1992.

Chapter 14

The Power of Truth

In part I, I described God-*rûah* as the motherly-and-fatherly energy which inspires all creation with expectation, power and fertility, the original power of love which vitally permeates the history of life in this universe and therefore the enduring power of resistance to the ever-present menace of chaotic upheaval.

The gospel of John refers to this *rûah* as the Spirit of truth. In John 16:13 Jesus calls the power of the risen Christ the "*pneuma* of truth" that will guide the disciples "into all the truth". John 8:32 tells us that this truth "will make you [Jesus' disciples] free". The first epistle of John insists that the *pneuma* of the Son of God is the truth (5:6).

Even these few citations show clearly that truth is an essential characteristic of *pneuma*. Everything the *rûah* does is truth, and therefore consistent in itself, univocal and unmistakable. There is no room for deceit or self-deception.

The systems and dispositions of life are inconceivable without truth and predictability. The Psalms are full of praise for God's truth. Grace and truth are like God's eyes watching over and maintaining the creation: "Your steadfast love, O Lord, extends to the heavens, your faithfulness [i.e., truth] to the clouds," says Psalm 36:5 (cf. Pss. 25:10; 89:14; 100:5; 115:1; 117:2). Paul's famous celebration of love in 1 Corinthians 13 also reminds us that love cannot develop without truth (v. 6).

These references point to a basic insight: what is central is not so much *telling* the truth as *being in* the truth. Thus when we pray to the Spirit as the Spirit of truth, we are praying to be so thoroughly suffused with truth that we too become truthful, reliable, straightforward, unambiguous. We are not asking for one virtue among others but for a particular way of being. Let us now look more closely at four aspects of being in the truth.

Accepting truth

The general direction is suggested by the verse from Psalm 36 cited above. Before all else, being in the truth means accepting the truth. That means saying Yes to the rhythms and arrangements by which creation develops. In so far as it is up to us, we try to recognize these excellent ordinances, not in order to exploit them but to admire their consistency and beauty. Praise of the Creator is the first utterance of the human spirit to emerge from perception of the truth. This kind of acceptance is a celebration of God's holy ordinances, a celebration that combines astonishment and admiration, awe and glorification. Thomas Berry underlines this when he says that we human beings should "renew our human participation in the grand liturgy of the universe".[1]

Accepting the truth does not mean merely acquiescing in the truth of our particular life, but embracing it with stout heart and level head. It is a matter of accepting not only our transience but our strengths and weaknesses, our fragility and our history. It is not easy to admit the truth of our particular existence, for we are always inclined to see ourselves inappropriately. We either despise or are enamoured of ourselves. We either mistreat or indulge ourselves. We willingly deceive ourselves about the depths of our lives, and most of the time we refuse to acknowledge the infirmity that tells us we are going to die.

Accepting the truth of God's ordinances in creation and in our personal life opens the door to thanksgiving. Thankfulness is closely linked to truth. It is a specific attitude of mind, a way of considering the miracles of our world and of remaining receptive to them. We shall return to this in the third part of this book when we look at the thankful, that is, eucharistic, celebration of thought about Jesus.

Being in the truth means thankful sharing in the celebration of the *rûah*, in and with the creation.

The struggle for an accurate view of reality

One of the stanzas of Rabanus Maurus' hymn addresses God's Spirit as the power that illuminates our minds: "Enable with perpetual light/ The dullness of our blinded sight". God's *pneuma* discloses itself in us as clarity of mind, as a quest for knowledge. Whereas truth in the mode of thankfulness contemplates its origin, truth in the mode of knowledge accompanies the Spirit in its work in creation.

Anyone who has done research knows the point of Paul's observation that this kind of knowledge is imperfect. "We know only in part" (1 Cor. 13:9). The more insights and data we are confronted with, the more difficult it is to obtain or retain an accurate image of our reality. Paradoxical as this may seem, the present world situation is to some extent so very hazardous precisely because we know too much about it. Phenomena are so complex that it seems impossible to obtain a consistent overall picture of them. The flood of information increases complexity to such a degree that a flexible yet integrated perception of reality is unattainable.

What does "being in the truth" mean under conditions of such complexity? First of all, it means that today no individual human being can master the task alone. Here we appreciate the meaning of the profoundly communal aspect of truth. No one possesses the truth for himself or herself alone. Rather, truth is something that asks to be communicated and imparted and seeks to be understood. Therefore we need working communities or groups in which we can discover and practise together the various methods of research and knowledge now available to us. I am thinking for example of the Club of Rome, which made it possible to obtain an overall view, and thus a kind of paradigm, of our complex world situation. In this process we obviously have to use the new possibilities afforded by information and computer science. And naturally such images of reality have to be constantly revised.

An authentic picture of reality can no longer be encyclopaedic. Instead, it must discern the rules and patterns of scientific, political, social and economic processes. No one would deny that this involves a study of the origins of these processes. What is less recognized is the need for a study of their foreseeable effects as well. Here it is a question of constantly restating predictable consequences. Unless we do that, we cannot keep up with the possible risks of complexity.

What I am pleading for is a communal — that is international and interdisciplinary — quest for an integrated picture of reality which includes awareness, elucidation and continuous revision of what has already happened. In this process, the specialization on which scientists always insist must be complemented by a concern for synthesis and cross-reference. Unfortunately, it is still thought to be a mark of scientific scholarship when an expert can exchange ideas on his or her speciality only with an increasingly smaller number of specialists. Today, however, a genuinely specialist knowledge must include a readiness and ability to offer information about the social, political and ethical implications of the particular area of knowledge involved.

Being in the truth also means that we have to associate with others in the search for a consistent and comprehensible image of reality. This requires us to leave the supposedly safe haven of our "expertise" in search of co-operative understanding. The low estimate in scientific circles of "generalists" and the disregard for "journalists" or "laypeople" interested in interpreting scientific knowledge in a way most people can understand is obsolete. The elucidation of dangerous complexity serves the life-potential of our world. Expert knowledge that rejects participation, sharing, ongoing discussion, questions and answers is irresponsible. Such a refusal to face the implications of responsibility can make it a form of deceptive and dominating knowledge.

Opposing the networks of lies

If courage and strength are involved in the struggle for an authentic image of reality, they are even more necessary for detecting and banishing the deceptive propaganda that makes it so difficult to discern the truth. We are faced not only with a fragmentation of knowledge but with ever-more deceptive constructs of the world situation.

For instance, now that the cold war has disappeared, we can see how much distortion and falsification lay behind the East-West opposition. People on both sides were victims of propaganda images of the other which made a realistic view of the situation impossible. The insanity of the arms race relied on our remaining deceivers deceived and deluders deluded.

The Gulf War in 1991 was conducted not only with sophisticated weapons but also with a skilful use of the communication media. Freedom of opinion and the press, fundamental pillars of a democratic society, were intentionally limited in order to deprive people, especially the citizens of the USA, of the truth about the reasons for the war and the extent of the devastation.[2] It was necessary to avoid what had happened during the Vietnam War, for unvarnished reporting had helped to bring that war to an end.

"The first casualty when war comes is truth." The accuracy of US Senator Hiram Johnson's often-quoted maxim of 1917 was cold-bloodedly confirmed during the Gulf War. Perhaps the truth might have set us free to promote not only an end to a disproportionate war but also a fundamentally different policy in that region of the world.

To my mind, the most convincing example of this deceptiveness is television. Throughout the third world, television manifests itself as the most subtle of all powers, for it introduces a distorted image of reality into the houses and shacks and thus the hearts and minds of the poor. Critical media education is extremely difficult in the affluent sectors of the societies of the North; in the increasingly impoverished regions of the world, where education is often only rudimentary, it seems well-nigh impossible. Soap operas and violent thrillers are essentially deceptive in themselves. But when this escapist programming is combined — in the slums of Bogota or Lagos, or in the tent of a semi-nomadic desert family — with advertising for products whose price makes them unattainable and government propaganda masquerading as news, an additional dimension of deception and confusion is created.

Television promotes a life that simply does not exist. After his travels through Latin America, Johann Baptist Metz affirmed:

> Religion is by no means the primary form of opium for the poor in Latin America. Today, it seems to me, that is the function of the mass-media culture which by now has forced its entry into the meanest *favelas*. It keeps the disadvantaged in an imaginary world of consumption and success. It alienates the poor from their own language... It robs them of their own memory... and makes them ineffectual as thinkers and actors in their own right.[3]

We have to combat lies, not only because they make it difficult to see reality as it is, but because they threaten to extinguish the light of reason, our very ability to perceive at all, and thus the strength of hope and renewal. But a lone individual is powerless against these systems, which soon render one silent and ineffectual. We can defend ourselves only by means of communal and ecumenical strategies against (self-)deception.

Enough people complain about the omnipotence and ubiquitousness of the mass media. Surely it is time for all communities that would live by the Spirit of truth to boycott these networks of lies. Being in the truth also means acting for the truth. This activity can also prove itself in conscious refusal to go along with things as they are.

Looking guilt in the eye

Finally, the *pneuma* of truth is also the power to accept the truth about our own lives in order to deal with the guilt and shame within us. It reveals moments when we are at odds with ourselves and guilty towards others.

Guilt is something that we try to dislodge from our minds but cannot get rid of. At the same time, our shame at injustices we have suffered can be so painful that we want to suppress it. We also suffer bitterly from weakness and self-hatred.

Therefore we live with ourselves in the twilight. We try to cover up certain parts of our nature and our past in order to enjoy a counterfeit peace. This applies not only to individuals but also to communities and countries. The histories of our nations include periods of doing great injustice, whether in destructive wars or in the persecution of minorities, other races and economically weaker classes. But those histories also comprise experiences of injustice suffered and harsh humiliation. A truthful examination of our history will reveal memories of guilt and of grievous wrongs.[4]

Into these dark areas the *pneuma* of truth casts a bright and often painful light, illuminating our history more profoundly. We become aware of what we have repeatedly refused to recognize: conflicts unreconciled, injustice unexpiated, errors and omissions accumulated, deceitful compromises and false peace.

* * *

To recapitulate: being in the truth means accepting and celebrating the ordinances and energies of creation. It also means recognizing lies, guilt and self-deception as harmful to life. Thus truth serves the well-being of creation. It is the light that we need in order constantly to rediscover the way of the peace of creation. The truth calls for and relies on a union with reason which is established in life itself by God-*rûah*.

Johann Gottfried Herder wrote that "reason is in the world... The more authentic it is, the more like itself this reason is in all thinking people, and the most genuine form of reason is certainly only one and the same."[5] Herder's words are redolent of the confidence in the power of *pneuma* which was the source of the European Enlightenment. The human spirit lives by the power and presence of the Spirit which always precedes it. The more genuine and authentic human reason is, the closer it comes to the universally reconciling power of divine reason.

But in saying this, Herder emphasizes another insight, the truth of which we have encountered repeatedly. The more authentic our exercise of the power of our reason, the better we are able to get along with others, because we can perceive and rediscover ourselves in their reasoning. Accordingly, because it makes understanding less difficult, truth is the power of straightforward simplicity. For that very reason it opposes the methods of deceitful simplification and propaganda and defies the strategies of confusion and lies.

Being in the truth, therefore, means being in the community of truth. The truth that God is produces a circle of illumination in which we begin to understand ourselves better and to resist systems of deception and lies more effectively.

NOTES

[1] *The Dream of the Earth*, San Francisco, 1988, p.215.
[2] Cf H. Graf, "Der Golfkrieg als mediale 'Bomberpoesie'", *Humboldt Journal für Friedensforschung*, Vol. 7, 1991, pp.57-61.
[3] J.B. Metz and H.E. Bahr, *Augen für die andern: Lateinamerika, eine theologische Erfahrung*, Munich, 1991, p.57.
[4] On the phenomenon of the history of guilt and offences against justice in the life of nations, see G. Müller-Fahrenholz, "On Shame and Hurt in the Life of Nations — a German Perspective", in *Studies: An Irish Quarterly*, Vol. 78, 31, 1989, pp.127-39.
[5] I am indebted for this reference to my colleague, Dr S. Reimers of Hamburg.

Chapter 15

The Power of Solidarity

The New Testament record

Of the New Testament passages which portray the divine *pneuma* as the power of consolation, the clearest are surely the so-called Farewell Discourses in the gospel of John, where Jesus promises his disciples the *parakletos*, the Paraclete or Comforter, after his death. It is important to realize that this Spirit of consolation is also the Spirit of truth (cf. John 14:16f.). The disciples will not be left "orphaned" (14:18). The *pneuma* of consolation will be a maternal and paternal power, a protective and homely power that will make of the disciples a new family of God.[1]

In John 14:26ff., the Paraclete is described as the power that keeps the memory of Jesus alive and enables people to reach a new understanding of his life and proclamation: "He will teach you everything, and remind you of all that I have said to you." This too is to be understood as a protective and supportive closeness, because we also know that it manifests the peace of Christ that preserves the human heart from fear and terror (cf. 14:27).

This line of thought is continued in John 15. There we learn that the disciples of Christ are to expect from the world the same hatred that their Master experienced (vv.18ff.). Such hostility is the inevitable lot of those who show the world its sinfulness. Here too the Comforter is revealed as the Spirit of truth (cf. 15:26; 16:13). There can be no doubt that the gospel of John also sees the community of the disciples with Jesus as sharing in his suffering. They must prepare for persecution, because they are entering a time of confusion so great that their enemies will think they can serve God by killing the people of Jesus (16:2), for this *pneuma* will "prove the world wrong about sin and righteousness and judgment" (16:8). But at the same time this divine power will bring the disciples great joy (cf. 16:22).

John's choice of birth-pangs as a metaphor for this struggle against the sins of the world is significant. He compares the pains of persecution with those a woman suffers when giving birth. These pains have a creative meaning: they accompany the coming forth of a new life and are forgotten as soon as the child is there — or rather they are swallowed up by the joy of having brought a human being into the world (16:21). In this context, then, God's *pneuma* represents consolation, for it gives suffering a meaning and makes it creative. Here we have to do not with the misfortune of unremitting futility but with a pain unavoidably associated with labour for the sake of new life and the promise of great joy.

The second beatitude may also be understood in this sense: "Blessed are those who mourn, for they will be comforted" (Matt. 5:4). Consolation is not something distant. It is intimately available to those who suffer with Jesus, because they are working in his Spirit for a new creation and thus elicit enmity and violent opposition. But this beatitude discloses another important perspective.[2] It does not forbid mourning; in fact, it encourages it. Jesus does not denounce the lamentation of those suffering bitterly under pain as cowardly whining, which should give way to stoic imperturbability. Rather, such a complaint expresses our search for other people: we cry out for community so that we can find some way to express our pain; and in this outpouring of pain we sometimes already have a foretaste of consolation and security.

Accordingly, consolation always implies support. I receive consolation from others. No one can comfort himself or herself. Consolation is the space which others open up to us and which gives us a chance to breathe anew when pain has taken our breath away. It is the caring hand that straightens the bruised reed and allows the dimly burning wick to flame up again (cf. Isa. 42:3). It is the encouraging voice or soothing embrace that awakens new endurance.

We find another perspective on all this in the second letter to the Corinthians,[3] which is a kind of compendium of Paul's confrontations with this community and reflects conflicting views of the right way to be an apostle and a true disciple of the crucified Jesus. Apparently, some forceful preachers had appeared in Corinth, claiming to be superior to Paul, who was "untrained in speech" and unassuming. In theological debate with these "super-apostles" (11:5; 12:11), Paul describes the nature of consolation as he has experienced it.

Paul speaks openly of his persecutions and sufferings, temptations and desperation, yet he knows that he is close to God despite all this. The doxology at the beginning of the letter speaks of God as the "Father of mercies and God of all consolation, who consoles us in all our affliction, so that we may be able to console those who are in any affliction with the consolation by which we ourselves are consoled by God" (1:3-4).

Tribulation and consolation are inseparable. Consolation is not the end of misery, but the power of assurance in the midst of all pain. In chapter 4 Paul makes this clear in a series of seemingly paradoxical statements which sum up the uniqueness of the kingdom of God amidst the riches of this world or, to put it another way, the uniqueness of consolation in the midst of distress: "We are afflicted in every way, but not crushed; perplexed, but not driven to despair; persecuted, but not forsaken; struck down, but not destroyed" (4:8ff.).

How can this be? Paul supplies the answer: We always carry "in the body the death of Jesus, so that the life of Jesus may also be made visible in our bodies" (4:10).

This is the dimension in which Paul sees his mission and that of the Christian communities. He does not talk of imitating the suffering of Christ. Instead, he is aware that he and all those baptized in Christ's name are incorporated into Christ. Through the *pneuma* the crucified and risen Lord is connected with his own people in a new body, and all those whom he calls share in his power, which seeks the cure and health of creation. For that reason they have to suffer the anger and hatred of God's enemies.

Paul clearly interprets the incomprehensible mystery of faith and discipleship as a power emanating from Jesus of Nazareth and joining Jews and pagans, women and men, free people and slaves in a new union (cf. Gal. 3:28). In spite of all barriers, this new community enables people to be one heart and one soul. In this body of Christ a new people, a new kingdom and a new creation come about, incarnate in the midst of a violent and self-destructive world.

This is the basis of consolation, and accordingly consolation is inseparable from the pain, conflict and humiliation constantly visited on the disciples of Jesus.

If we think of consolation as the protective and encouraging energy of the body of Christ, we realize why Paul sees "consolation" and "exhortation" as one and the same thing. The Greek word *parakletos* is generally rendered nowadays as "Intercessor", "Comforter" or Spirit of consolation, whereas the related term *paraklesis* is often translated "exhortation". While closely linked in Greek, these terms have tended to drift apart in English and several other modern European languages, which has affected our perception of the associated concepts, of course.

In general we do not link the exhortations of the Pauline letters with consolation but think of them as moralizing and even oppressive reprimands. It is thus important to realize that the energy of consolation is a constructive power. This association is more obvious if we look to the Latin word for *consolatio*, with its echoes of the word *solidus*, "genuine", "solid", "sterling", "authentic". Consolation thus has the connotation of enabling people to keep their feet on the ground, pointing them in an authentic, trustworthy direction. Since this is a communal, corporate form of caring, it includes a concern for solid structures and communal order. The *paraklesis* of Paul can then be seen as his contribution to solid communal arrangements of service that help to ensure that God's creative *pneuma*, which sustains the creation and restrains chaos, is powerfully effective in the life and work of the children of God.

Of course, this can happen only within the changing historical circumstances in which we live. Therefore Paul's *paraklesis* is never to be interpreted as a law for all times and situations. He told his churches what he thought and found to be consoling, "edifying" and constructive for authentic discipleship of Jesus. But precisely because the *pneuma* of consolation is creative and alive, each generation has to work on and for the *paraklesis* that is consoling, edifying and constructive for its own time. A mere repetition of what has gone before would be fundamentalist.

In this context it is noteworthy that *paraklesis* and charisms are closely associated in Pauline theology. The *pneuma* of God is present and seeks expression in these gifts, the criterion for which is the *oikodomé*, the constructive encouragement of community. Charisms originate in God's *charis*, God's grace. Hence they are kenotic forms of thankfulness, and should never serve the purposes of self-glorification, lest they lose their character as grace and lead to divisions and dissension in church communities. The life of communities is established on a solid basis in the equal entitlement and co-operation of charisms (cf. 1 Cor. 14:3ff.).

Something of the constructive implications of the Latin *solidus* is retained in the English word "solidarity". To be sure, this word has been overused in some circles and is suspect in others because of its association with trade unions and left-wing political organizations. Nevertheless, it has connotations no longer available in the word "consolation", particularly in underscoring the aspects of community and active commitment. We show solidarity when we support one another, set one another on the right path, stand up on one another's behalf, protect, take care of and, as necessary, criticize one another. Solidarity implies the constructive communal association which is fundamental in the New Testament but has vanished from the bourgeois notion of consolation.

Consolation devalued

With great respect and profundity, the ancient Christian Pentecost hymns refer to the Creator Spirit as the Consoler or Comforter. To return to the words of Rabanus Maurus (in Cosin's version):

> *Thy blessed Unction from above,*
> *Is comfort, life and fire of love.*
> *Enable with perpetual light,*
> *The dullness of our blinded sight.*

Here the consoling Spirit is something precious, a source of life, love and fire, a medicine that God gives us for the sake of our health. The hymn conveys a precise awareness of the great extent of our need. Without this consoling power, we are like sick and blinded people.

How could the word "consolation", with its obvious basic significance for the life of Christian communities, become false, valueless and indeed misleading for us today? How has it come to suggest little more than "cheering someone up", a cheap and indulgent exercise in "calming someone down", a pious pose devoid of gravity and depth? I think there are three main reasons for this devaluation.

1. *The privatization of consolation.* Whereas the New Testament teaches us that consolation is a vital expression of the Spirit, the most profound sustaining force of the body of Christ, it has become in our churches something private. Withdrawal into the private chamber of individualism has affected not only prayer and intercession but also pastoral care, which has become a personal affair, even a private concern. Pastors have begun to think of themselves as personal advisors and counsellors. This has led to a suppression or dissipation of what Paul sees as *paraklesis* —

working to achieve in the community a way of life that serves the peace of creation. Anything that resembles "parish visiting" has become obsolete. In Roman Catholic circles pastoral theology has retained its original sense, combining pastoral care and nurture of the parish, though of course that does not guarantee that the function of consolation is preserved in the full biblical sense.

An example of this loss of significance is found in penance. It is evident that the practice of confession has almost disappeared from Protestantism, but even in Catholicism the sacrament of penance has become a pious practice from which scarcely anyone expects true consolation anymore. If penance ever was the edification of the individual within a setting of communal consciousness-raising, there is hardly any trace of that today.

The pastoral consultation has become increasingly removed from any critical and constructive aspect and the element of serving and strengthening community has diminished. It has become a "counselling session". Pastoral care has in turn been transformed into pastoral psychology. On a professional level, this change has meant that "the cure of souls" as part of the pastor's office has been replaced by the self-sufficient vocation of the pastoral psychologist. Moreover, the special bent for pastoral care of many ministers, both men and women, leads them to attend courses and obtain qualifications that gradually enable them to abandon the parish as the proper locus of pastoral care. Many now work as psychotherapists with their own practices.

Without denying the significance of the work they do, one can see two tendencies being mutually reinforced as a result. On the one hand, consolation as the expression of communal solidarity has vanished; on the other hand, the prestige of the psychotherapist, who works mainly with individuals, has grown, encouraging a decline in the significance of traditional pastoral care. A consequence of this professionalization is that people begin to mistrust the charism of solidarity between human beings and make it a professional concern.

As a result, there is no longer any realization that consolation or solidarity is a sign of God's presence and that all work in this area can express practical pneumatology and must retain its association with the *ecclesia* as the community of disciples of the crucified and resurrected Lord.

2. *Consolation misunderstood as therapy.* That "consolation" means very little to us nowadays is also due to a misunderstanding

already apparent in the lines of Rabanus Maurus cited above. He speaks of the Holy Spirit, the Comforter, as *spiritalis unctio* — in Cosin's paraphrase the "blessed unction from above", but literally "spiritual salve". The Holy Spirit is portrayed as a medicine for sickness and disease. Undoubtedly the *pneuma* of consolation has something to do with healing and liberation. But contrary to a widespread idea, consolation is not an ointment that helps us to recover from a specific sickness. We speak of a "problem" that is "solved" after one or several counselling sessions. We experience a loss that we are said to have "got over" after consolation. Such hastily offered encouraging and comforting remarks may constitute false consolation precisely because they are mere "consoling words" when what is really needed is protective, patient solidarity.

We have seen that for Paul consolation is the protective power in the midst of the struggle for the kingdom of God. It is not a matter of "solving" certain "problems" — indeed there are psychotherapists available for that — but of life in the power of solidarity, which helps us to endure temptation, doubt, persecution and suffering for the sake of the kingdom of God.

3. *Consolation without truth.* The gospel of John teaches us that there is no consolation without truth. Yet, people often act as if consolation is fostered precisely by avoiding the truth. Confused with easy optimism, consolation is reduced to the level of deceitful, false or hypocritical talk.

Any pastor will know of cases in which he or she has been expected to offer consolation without telling the truth. That happens not only when someone has died, though as the old saying has it, there are never so many lies told as at funerals. I can recall, for example, discussions with representatives of firms, banks or political parties in which critical questions about investments in apartheid South Africa were countered with the argument: "You people in the church should spend your time comforting others rather than sticking your nose in our affairs!" When injustice is concealed and deceit is not mentioned by name, consolation becomes an hypocritically deceitful manoeuvre. But God's *pneuma* brings consolation only as truth, and truth only as consolation.[4]

Our reflections on three common ways in which the concept of consolation has been devalued show the urgent need to recover the authentic dimension of consolation and of solidarity. Despite all our objections to cheap consolation, we may not ignore the extent to which solidarity is absent from this world. What I have said about widespread joylessness, cynicism, fundamentalism and violentism also represents a grievous history of helplessness and desperation.

We cannot show real concern regarding the truth of our historical reality, the devastating threats of our time, the degree of systematic deception and the demonic depths of error, inadequacy and guilt, without simultaneously seeking the power of consolation and solidarity. Without this protective, stabilizing and encouraging force we would despair of the fruitfulness of truth. Only if we come to our senses, only with consolation, can the truth set us free.

NOTES

[1] On this chapter as a whole, see V. Weymann, *Trost? Orientierungsversuch zur Seelsorge*, Zurich, 1989; on this paragraph in particular, K. Wengst, *Bedrängte Gemeinde und verherrlichter Christus: Ein Versuch über das Johannes-Evangelium*, 3rd ed., Munich, 1990.

[2] Cf. Weymann, *op. cit.*, pp.31ff. (following Hans Weder).

[3] *Ibid.*, pp.67ff.

[4] It must not be forgotten, however, that when politicians or industrialists remind us of the church's duty of consolation, there may be more than a defensive interest at work. They could be expressing a need for real consolation and solidarity. Church criticism of the powerful, particularly coming from grassroots communities, does often tend to overlook the real difficulties and crises they are in.

Chapter 16

The Power of Endurance

The word "faithful" is rich with associations. A faithful worker is one who is reliable and steadfast on the job, yet neither obstinate nor mechanical. A faithful marriage partner remains tender and attentive without becoming hard or uncaring. Faithful individuals carry out their duties but are never fanatically obsessed by them. Faithfulness presupposes consistency, flexibility and truthfulness. It develops from profound self-esteem and from an assurance of support and security.

Steadfast faithfulness in the New Testament

We find the adjective "faithful" (*pistós*) in the New Testament but not the noun "faithfulness". But if we look for descriptions of faithfulness in action, this apparent gap is filled.

First of all, we encounter the verb *menein*, "abide" or "remain", which plays a major part in the Johannine writings. A few textual references suffice to show that the notion of "abiding" establishes the lasting relationship between Jesus and his disciples as firmly as the unshakable relationship between Jesus and his Father. "Abide in me as I abide in you," we read in the parable of the true vine (John 15:4). "Abide in my love" is found in various contexts (John 15:9; cf. 1 John 4:16).

This abiding is not a matter of passive waiting, merely "sitting it out", but an active, resolute concern for an inward relationship. To abide in love means loving, staying receptive, empathizing with others, remaining flexible regarding their strengths and weaknesses, always ready to help and to receive. Abiding is central to living, constantly renewed interactions. Such an unceasing relationship characterizes Jesus' closeness to his Father and to his community. That is the power of the Spirit, the sign of the presence of the *pneuma*. We "abide" in the space of this *pneuma*. Henri Nouwen writes: "Jesus, in whom God's fullness dwells, is our home... By choosing us as his preferred home, he invites us to choose him as our own dwelling. That is the mystery of the Incarnation."[1]

Menein also takes the related form *hypomenein* ("to abide among") with the associated noun *hypomone*, sometimes translated "patience". Here we encounter further difficulties. "Patience" can suggest passivity, even lack of initiative. Being patient often implies just waiting to see what will happen. Patience is not always a positive term. We remember as children having our anticipations of something pleasant dashed when an adult told us, "Be patient!" We may hear the same from pious believers, even pastors, who cannot think of anything other to say than "Be patient!" when we have suffered something unbearable.

We must forget all these negative connotations when enquiring into the meaning of the Greek *hypomone* today. It is much closer to what we understand as endurance, an idea that plays a central role in Paul's letters. In Romans 15:5 God is called the "God of steadfastness and encouragement"; in 2 Corinthians 1:3 the "Father of mercies and God of all consolation". The biblical meaning might better be conveyed as the "God of endurance and solidarity". The supportive, protective God of solidarity is full of *hypomone*, that is, enduring, untiring, unshakable in his consoling presence.

This recalls again what we said earlier about *creatio continua*, continuous creation. The power of the constant renewal of creation, the energy of unflagging resistance to the powers of chaos is *hypomone*: abiding in lovingkindness while bearing the burden of having to sustain life and displaying a combative devotion to the earth. This is endurance: steadfastness, the power of persistence and knowing where one is going.

We may thus speak of the *pneuma* as the power of endurance. It is of central importance to the life of Christian communities because it evokes the dimension of steadfastness and persistence. This is also unmistakable in the derivatives of the Latin *perseverantia* in English and the Romance languages. Our life and practice should also be permeated with this endurance. Without it we neither bring forth fruit (cf. Luke 8:15) nor take part in and win the inevitable struggle (cf. Heb. 12:1; 1 Cor. 9:24ff.).

This kind of endurance is referred to at many points in the New Testament. I shall cite only two aspects that seem especially relevant in the present context: endurance in prayer and endurance in suffering.

Endurance in prayer

Anyone reading the Pauline letters immediately notices that they begin by praising God and interceding on behalf of the churches.[2] Paul practises what he recommends to the churches: constancy in prayer (cf. Rom. 12:12; Col. 4:2). Intercession is an act of loyal remembrance, in which the "unity of the Spirit in the bond of peace" is maintained and constantly renewed.

What happens when we intercede for one another? By interceding we contribute to the network of constant remembrance and participation that has extended over the globe since people first started praying. This network keeps alive people whom others want to silence and ignore. Intercession is a vital bridge to all who are being tortured, held in sound-proof cells or otherwise kept *incommunicado*. The persecuted and prisoners are people torn from our memories. Intercession communicates a power to encourage all those who risk losing their minds in the loneliness of their cells and under the burden of isolation. Intercession infiltrates networks of propaganda and resists their stultifying influence. It opposes the invention of distorted images of our opponents and the portrayal of people, nations and races as enemies. It undermines injustice. By remembering the suffering and disadvantaged, it trains the spotlight of critical public opinion on the agents of violence and oppressors. Through endurance in intercession, truth and consolation prevail in their own right.

Endurance in suffering

Endurance in suffering is directly linked with endurance in prayer. All the New Testament writings are marked by the experience of suffering to one extent or another. In regions governed by the *Pax Romana*, those who embraced the *Pax Christi* could expect only oppression, contempt and tribulation. How tempting it must have been to escape from these tormented minorities and to join the big battalions! The other dangerous temptation was to take refuge in gnostic sects.

The New Testament communities are portrayed as resistance groups. The primary reason for this was not that historically the Roman Empire was irreconcilable with the gospel of Jesus Christ. Rather, in the *Pax Romana* system the first Christian communities recognized a world order that was diametrically opposed to the peace of Christ. What they had acknowledged as the peace of creation could not be reconciled with the violence of this "peaceful order". The light of the new creation plainly revealed the transience of this world. Adaptation was impossible. Constructive resistance was the order of the day. The early Christians had to be very careful when deciding what to take over. The spirits had to be tested meticulously to see if they were of God (cf. 1 John 4:1). Faithfulness to Christ and his kingdom was of central importance for an attentive and loving life prepared for self-sacrifice. Without such endurance, any kind of resistance would soon founder.

All over the world many Christians clearly feel that their own conditions of life are remarkably similar to those under which the first Christian communities had to suffer. What happened to people in Palestine and Asia Minor — the impoverishment of the little people and above all of children, the corrupt collaboration of the local upper classes with the central Roman power, the imposition of new gods and of education in violence by means of murderous sports in the arena — sounds strangely contemporary. What we today call the third world lives under similar conditions. It too is on the periphery. Its countries are deprived of power, and the fruits of their labour fill the markets of the rich world. While the mass of little people is becoming gradually more impoverished and an increasingly large number of children waste their wretched lives on the streets of large cities, the cliques of the powerful gratify themselves ever more openly with their unjust wealth. In the midst of all this, many television and film producers have assumed the role of the Roman arena, setting up a "school" of violence and apathy in which it is precisely the poorest of the poor who are offered as defenceless prey. It is difficult to remain steadfast under such conditions.

Endurance in time

Endurance in intercession and endurance in suffering are — though for opposite reasons — difficult to maintain. Many people find the former too easy and the latter too difficult. Activist groups sometimes treat as false mysticism the suggestion that intercession is a far-reaching power of *pneuma*. Some communities that have grown used to comfort think it is asking too much to expect a Christian life to prove itself by resisting the world's unjust systems.

But intercession is no easy exercise of piety. Instead it demands a refined political awareness, a dedicated study of secret injustice and an undaunted readiness to stand up and speak out in public. In this sense, Amnesty International and Action of Christians for the Abolition of Torture (ACAT) are two examples of worldwide support organizations whose endurance deserves admiration.

But all these forms of endurance are grounded in a more fundamental certainty which I would call trust in the endurance of time.

The "numbing" and despair which take so many forms today conceal a deep mistrust of the reliability of time. No longer do we see the future as the unquestionably secure space into which we can project ourselves, for it is itself under the threats of ecological and nuclear disaster. Such threats are also reflected in the impossibility of enduring, resisting, being reliable and striving for a goal. We become apathetic and depend on the support of our drugs — of which alcohol, cocaine, pills and television are only among the most powerful. We may become as reckless and changeable as Proteus, the god of many shapes and disguises, and as excitable as we are oblivious. Or we may turn to sour fundamentalism and cling to self-justifying "eternal verities".

A basic dejection lies behind all this. The current of time no longer bears us along. This is expressed as an exhaustion of vital energies, as despair under the guise of depression, as a lack of vitality and joy in life. But God's creation energy unfolds in endurance. It is the vitality that enables our lives to reflect God's faithful, untiring fullness of life. This ongoing process of coming to be and shaping power forbids apocalyptic despair. Because God lives and because this life is creation and love, time has meaning, basis and extent.

It is in the house of God's faithfulness that our endurance finds its proper dwelling-place. It offers truth and solidarity the support of a long, deep breath. It is in endurance that truth and solidarity find their direction and lasting power. In the vitality of constancy they also remain vital, creative and new every day.

NOTES

[1] H.R.W. Nouwen, *Im Hause des Lebens*, 3rd ed., Freiburg im Breisgau, 1986, p.30.
[2] Cf. L. Vischer, *Intercession*, Geneva, 1980, pp.40ff.

Chapter 17

Truth, Solidarity and Endurance as a Paradigm of Pastoral Theology

Prophet, priest, king

Every page of the New Testament testifies to the reality of *pneuma*. The Pauline letters have much to say about the "fruits" of *pneuma*. Romans 14:17 presents the triad justice or righteousness, peace and joy. Galatians 5:22 lists the fruit of the Spirit as "love, joy, peace, patience, kindness, generosity, faithfulness, gentleness and self-control".

Our own terms "truth", "solidarity" and "endurance" do not refer to typical "fruits" of the Spirit but to pneumatological dimensions that go into a paradigm of pastoral theology. Here we have a model of understanding and action that includes the fundamental characteristics of *pneuma* and offers the basic elements of an ecumenical pastoral theology. These dimensions of *pneuma* are interactive and each is incomplete without the others.

Truth is an inclusive term for the critical, discriminatory dimension. In truth, God's *pneuma* is communicated as penetrating, testing, analytical reason, as the driving force of intellectual knowledge and the unwavering power to reveal error and guilt.

Solidarity captures the synthetic, constructive dimension. Here *pneuma* is shown as the power of comfort, encouragement and reconciliation.

Endurance stands for the prospective dimension. Here *pneuma* appears as the combative, persistent power that offers support throughout the ages and as the energy of resistance that guarantees the eschatological openness of the future.

Accordingly, this threefold paradigm offers a union of rational and emotional energy in the medium of a time that is open, not apocalyptically restricted. Truth without solidarity and endurance would make us dogmatic, cold and unfeeling. Solidarity without truth and endurance would be hypocritical — uplifting but ineffectual words. Endurance without truth and solidarity would necessarily turn hard and fanatical. Together, however, they form a life-promoting creative field in which our life can develop. Truth offers the orientation, solidarity the support, endurance the long breath. The senses of truth enable us to perceive what is happening. The senses of solidarity allow us to communicate with one another and with the ground that bears us. The senses of endurance set us to work.

When these three are united, joy, wisdom and peace result. They form a complementary and perichoretic whole — the Christological emphasis we find in exemplary and prototypical form in Jesus of Nazareth.

It is as the witness to truth that Jesus becomes Christ, the anointed one and Son of God, for us. The gospels insist that Jesus' mandate consists precisely in his proclamation of truth. As the authentic witness, he confronts the political and religious powers and reveals their hypocrisy and essential duplicity. He knows the minds of human beings and can tell them the truth about their lives. He sees into their guilty deviousness, realizes the misery from which they suffer and liberates them. He scrutinizes and illuminates history prophetically and summons people to change their lives.

As the guarantor of truth, Jesus is also the *"consolation of Israel"*, as he is welcomed by old Simeon (Luke 2:25). In him, the aged and infirm find their merciful physician and healer. He gives women and children the dignity they were — and are — deprived of. He offers a new community to all those who are torn from their familiar surroundings by his summons of truth. A new family of the children of God forms about him. Thus, as the Son of the *rûah*, Jesus is not only the consolation of Israel but the comforter of all who are poor, abandoned and rejected.

Jesus is their *faithful guardian*. He continues undaunted on his way, though beset by temptations and enmity. He assumes the suffering of others. His agonizing, undignified death on the cross brings him the anguish of distance from God, but he remains faithful and trustworthy even at the cost of abandonment by God.

As the Word of truth, as the consolation of the world and the faithful guarantor of the kingdom, Jesus of Nazareth reveals himself to us as the Son of God, as the Son of the *rûah*, as Spirit in person. In the three complementary dimensions of his life's service, we recognize once again what Calvin called the prophetic, priestly and royal office of Christ. Just as it is impossible to separate these three modes of action in Christ, so we may not wrench them apart in the life of the Christian community. Prophetic truth, priestly solidarity and kingly endurance endow the pastoral theological paradigm we need with a powerful and passionate vitality.

A critical element

Our threefold paradigm also has a critical element, and although it cannot be described in detail here, I shall outline certain aspects of it:

1. The pneumatological basis of the paradigm of truth, solidarity and endurance guards against the danger of separating pastoral psychological projects and programmes from their theological ground. There is a desperate need for therapy in our world because of the amount and extent of anxiety, meaninglessness and loneliness. But if we see this need for therapy as a theological and church undertaking, it becomes part of life in the *pneuma*, which opens up an entirely new view of the world and of humankind. It is also important to note that once we grasp this need for therapy, major critical questions arise regarding the conduct of everyday parish and community life.

2. The pastoral theological paradigm proposed here runs counter to the individualization of pastoral care, which is directed to the welfare of the individual or of the group and neglects the social and cosmic aspects of the problem as well as actual political conditions. When psychological and group dynamics efforts become a kind of subculture where we can come to terms with ourselves without really being in the world, life in the dynamics of the *pneuma* is betrayed.

3. Consequently, it is important to integrate the emotional, somatic and affective forces of our life into our pastoral theology, despite the discouragement of this strategy by those who are suspicious of intellectual and rational energies. We have to use our reflective powers to the full if we are to see reality clearly and appropriately.

4. We must not forget that those who stress the emotional and somatic aspects of the question are often reacting to an over-intellectualized form of theology, and that this can happen in pastoral theology too. Moreover, where liberation theology still prevails, I have observed a tendency to prefer intellectual "analyses" of the social situation and to downplay the affective and somatic aspects of pastoral theology and care. It is not surprising that in Latin America, for example, Pentecostal and evangelical preachers should fill this gap.

5. "Unreflective anthropocentrism" is a charge levelled against both individualizing approaches to pastoral theology and those with an interest in social and political conditions. I have insisted on the creation aspect of the biblical proclamation of God's *pneuma* in order to stress that every form of pastoral theology today must discover its field of application in the *oikos* of creation. The peace of the soul, peace among human beings and peace between nations can thrive only when rooted in peace with creation.

* * *

At the end of part I, I said that the revelation of Jesus Christ discloses a comprehensive historical myth concerning the profound association between creation and redemption, between the history of the world and salvation history. I then referred to the psychological expression of this historically open myth in the process of symbolization and imagination, in "work on immortality". We find the theological basis of this vision of the collective continuity of life in the divine *pneuma*, in which creative and constructive energies are joined with the forces of loving self-sacrifice in all forms of being.

The paradigm of truth, endurance and solidarity is grounded in this vision. We turn now to the practice derived from it.

Part III
Creator Spirit
Soul of Christian Communities

Chapter 18

Ecodomy — Building the House of Life

The 17th-century German poet Andreas Gryphius described the Spirit as "the word by which God has built the house of the earth". For him "house of the earth" was a metaphor for the goodness and solidity of God's creative work; at the end of the 20th century this term starkly evokes the challenge facing humanity: to keep the earth alive. Ecology has taught us that our planet is indeed one single *oikos*, a house whose ecosystems interact in marvellously intricate ways to ensure the functioning of one global "biosphere".[1]

In fact, we are finding it exceedingly difficult to learn this lesson. Over thousands of years the human race has been trained to fight for itself in small social units in a world that appeared to be an endless, overpowering and inexhaustible expanse "out there". Even though we have seen photographs of our planet taken by astronauts, which make it look like a small and precious thing lost in the expanses of the universe, our everyday experience still convinces us that the world is vast, "enormous" in the original sense of the term — outside every conceivable norm — and beyond human control. To this day economics operates this way. Even multinational corporations that operate around the globe presuppose that nature is infinitely capable of absorbing every human folly. Recognizing that the preservation of the integrity of the biosphere must be given highest priority is thus a struggle against deep-seated beliefs. We must recapture the original sense of the term "economics" as the art of administering the global household. The "house of the earth" must remain intact if our little homes are to have a future.

The paradigm of *dominating* the earth which has guided most of human activity over the millennia needs to be replaced by the paradigm of *inhabiting* the earth, which aims at establishing compatible and sustaining forms of interaction between humans and nature. We need new visions for global "household politics".[2]

In this connection the Greek word *oikodomé* takes on considerable significance. In its literal sense it refers to the building of a house, but its meaning can be extended to any constructive process. So the apostle Paul uses this word for the building up of Christian communities. He calls his apostolic mission a service to the *oikodomé* of Christ (2 Cor. 13:10). He reminds members of Christian communities that they should behave towards each other in the spirit of *oikodomé* (Rom. 14:19). They are called to use their specific gifts and talents (charisms) for the *oikodomé* of the Body of Christ (Eph. 2:21), just as they are reinforced and strengthened by the pneumatic energy of this body.

This concept of "ecodomy" can inspire our search for a politics for the "house of the earth". Its forward-looking connotations encourage the search for innovative visions and suggest the quality of creative constructiveness. For communities do not "grow" like plants; they need to be planned, shaped, nurtured, organized, corrected and, if necessary, dismantled and rebuilt. Ecodomy denotes an activity which presupposes hope and confidence. It is eschatology put to practice.

The apostle Paul regarded the early Christian churches as "ecodomical centres" that were related to each other across deep cultural and religious barriers. What the letter to the Ephesians calls "the unity of the Spirit in the bond of peace" (4:3) could well be understood as an *ecodomical* covenant. Although tiny and weak, these centres saw themselves as part of a movement of liberation and reconstruction with cosmic dimensions. The risen Christ was not just the new human being, he was a cosmic reality, the first fruit of a new creation. To belong to this new realm empowered the early Christians to confront the brutal reality of the Roman Empire to the point of enduring martyrdom.

But the early Christian church did not develop this ecodomical perspective; instead, it settled for another concept also derived from the word *oikos*: that is, *paroikía*. This word means literally "living away from home". It is understandable that some of these small and persecuted Christian groups began to see themselves as communities of "aliens and exiles" in a hostile world, whose true homeland was in the heavens (cf. 1 Pet. 2:11). Eventually each local Christian church came to be called *paroikía*, a home away from home, as it were, a place of refuge. The "parochial system" became the organizing principle around which the church was set up. So the church was *in* the world, but not *of* the world.

Christians were taught to regard the earth as an alien place, full of evil spirits and powers, a "vale of tears" (which of course it often was), and to put all their hope in the heavenly home. Obviously, this helped to foster a dualism which despised the earth and glorified the world beyond.

There is an undeniable tension between *oikodomé* and *paroikía*. Whereas the former implies purpose and creativity, the latter tends towards separation of earth and heaven and fosters an escapist spirituality. But this need not be the case. The notion of *paroikía* is useful in underscoring that the followers of Christ can only be strangers in a world that rejects him. "How could we sing the Lord's song in a foreign land?" This sigh of Psalm 137:4 reflects the painful reality that God-fearing people can never be at home in a godless world. Yet legitimate as this lament is, it does not warrant our ceasing to sing the Lord's song. In other words, the notions of *oikodomé* and *paroikía* must be connected. The constructive and immanent thrust of ecodomical communities must incorporate the element of critical nonconformity. Ecodomical communities cannot be at peace with the violent powers that threaten to throw the world into chaos; rather, they must seek to correct and transform a world in crisis.

How can the churches regain this original passion for ecodomical transformation when "parochial" thinking has been the leading paradigm in the history of Christianity? We should note in the first place that the parochial system was intimately linked with close church-state relations and that it is losing ground everywhere, even in traditional state-churches in Europe. All Constantinian models of church and state are breaking apart. Christian communities across the globe have to cope with the painful reality that they are in a minority. Moreover, as we saw earlier, Christians in many parts of the world have discovered frightening similarities between their life and that of the early churches under Roman rule. Discipleship never ceases to be costly.

But even in contexts that are not hostile to Christian communities, the very conditions of modern societies — the impact of mobility, urbanization and the media for instance — have brought the traditional parochial system under considerable stress. Congregational structures clearly continue to have an important function, especially in relation to families, neighbourhoods and local community life. But more flexible expressions of Christian witness also need to be developed to meet the needs and demands of the mobile communities of business and banking, science and technology, global communication media and mass tourism.

My suggestion is that parochial thinking be transformed in the light of the possibilities opened up by the concept of ecodomy. We should understand our congregational units and mobile groups as ecodomical centres which respond to the demands of modern life by forming ecodomical networks or covenants. Just as the earth's ecosystems communicate with each other by virtue of their diversity, so our ecodomical centres and groups must learn to communicate with each other. They need to make creative use of their diversities rather than to see them as tools for defending their "confessional identity". The great wealth of theological, liturgical and spiritual traditions ought to be considered as charisms for the building up and well-being of this one household earth. It is through such sharing that Christian communities can become the "salt of the earth" and the leaven of the bread that keeps people alive.

I am convinced that we are only at the beginning of what can truly be called an ecumenical movement, even though some people predict its imminent demise. The ecumenical structures that have emerged in the 20th century are only a first stage. If stagnation has set in, the main reason is that hitherto attempts have been made to merge two obsolete organizational models: the traditional church pattern as it has developed historically in its denominational and cultural location; and the global principle of transnational companies.

The decisive question is whether the churches are facing up to the challenge that they too are subject to epochal transformations. Will they begin to understand that they are in fact part of one single system? Will they appreciate that they are all dependent on the life-sustaining breath of God's *pneuma* and that their calling is to join to become partners in God's ecodomy? Many people in the ecumenical movement are aware that we are already involved in a radical shift of paradigm.[3] To be sure, there are also many who react to such changes defensively and apologetically. But this is a clear indication that the crisis is felt; the time for radical changes is at hand.

I am certain that this paradigm-shift requires the churches to understand the ecumenical movement as an invitation to enter into an ecodomical covenant. In the following chapters, I shall try to elicit the implications of such a perspective in the light of what I have already said about truth, solidarity and endurance. The task is to show the implications of this pastoral paradigm for the communal life of the churches.

In order to be as specific as possible I shall refer to the work of the World Council of Churches and especially to its conciliar process for Justice, Peace and the Integrity of Creation. There are two reasons for selecting this particular case study. In the first place, the World Council of Churches, though it by no means includes all Christian churches and communities, represents the most extensive form of alliance among Christian churches. It is the most realistic reflection of the circumstances in which Christian communities find themselves in the rich and poor regions of the world. Therefore it also portrays the tensions and difficulties within and between these communities in an honest way. No other ecumenical organization has this representative character. Second, the conciliar process for Justice, Peace and Integrity of Creation is an initiative that has fixed its sights on the basic tasks of our time. This is not only an ethical programme; it is also concerned with the question of what it means to the church of Christ today. This process is thus uniquely suited to explore how truth, solidarity and endurance must interact in order to give the concept of ecodomy its full spiritual dimension.

NOTES

[1] Cf. Jeremy Rifkin, *Biosphere Politics: A Cultural Odyssey from the Middle Ages to the New Age*, San Francisco, 1991.
[2] An illuminating example is offered by E.U. von Weizsäcker, *Erdpolitik: Ökologische Realpolitik an der Schwelle zum Jahrhundert der Umwelt*, Darmstadt, 1989.
[3] Cf. Konrad Raiser, *Ecumenism in Transition: A Paradigm Shift in the Ecumenical Movement?*, Geneva, 1991.

Chapter 19

The Spirit of Truth at Work in the Ecodomical Covenant

The context of the case study

In 1983 delegates to the sixth assembly of the World Council of Churches (WCC) in Vancouver, Canada, approved "Justice, Peace and Integrity of Creation" (JPIC) as one of the priorities for the Council's programmes in the years ahead. Since then JPIC has received considerable attention and interest in member churches and beyond.

In setting forth this priority the Vancouver assembly formulated the notion of a "conciliar process", which would enable the churches to approach these global ethical problems in a meaningful way. The term "conciliar process" refers back to a major discussion launched by the WCC's Faith and Order Commission a decade earlier, which had led to a declaration on the nature of church unity at the WCC's fifth assembly in Nairobi in 1975. The one church, it declared, is to be

> envisioned as a conciliar fellowship of local churches which are themselves truly united. In this conciliar fellowship, each local church possesses, in communion with the others, the fullness of catholicity, witnesses to the same apostolic faith, and therefore recognizes the others as belonging to the same church of Christ and guided by the same Spirit... They are bound together because they have received the same baptism and share in the same eucharist; they recognize each other's members and ministries. They are one in their common commitment to confess the gospel of Christ by proclamation and service to the world. To this end, each church aims at maintaining sustained and sustaining relationships with her sister churches, expressed in conciliar gatherings whenever required for the fulfilment of their common calling.[1]

The term "conciliar" refers back to the great councils of the early church, which served to solve doctrinal disputes and establish binding formulas and procedures for all Christians. The call for conciliar gatherings in both Nairobi and Vancouver expressed the longing of Christian communities for a great council that would give guidance on the profound problems that plague humanity today.

The idea that emerged from Vancouver in this context did meet with a certain resistance, above all from the Orthodox churches, which thought of conciliarity as something intimately associated with the unity of the church. For Orthodoxy a council of separated churches is a contradiction in terms, and the notion of a "conciliar process" is misleading.

Nevertheless, the proposal of the Vancouver assembly was welcomed with considerable though varying enthusiasm. In 1989 the churches of the still-divided Europe followed up the Vancouver recommendation with their own assembly in the ancient conciliar city of Basel. For the first time since the Reformation, representatives of the Orthodox, Roman Catholic and Protestant churches met together. This encounter resulted in a common document with specific proposals that have undoubtedly influenced the tumultuous changes that have since taken place on that continent.[2]

Elsewhere in the world reaction to the Vancouver initiative was not as rapid. In March 1990, however, a world convocation for Justice, Peace and the Integrity of Creation was held in Seoul, South Korea. In order to circumvent the resistance to the word "council" the somewhat artificial name "convocation" was used as a way of avoiding a problematical term while retaining the essential intention of making declarations and eliciting commitments of a more binding nature than could be expected from normal conferences. It was hoped that these might lead to a new kind of common practice on the part of the churches.

In 1991 the seventh assembly of the World Council of Churches in Canberra expressly affirmed that the common search for justice, peace and the integrity of creation must remain a basic concern of the ecumenical movement. The assembly also agreed on a new statement on "the unity of church as koinonia", which was clearly intended to lead beyond the Nairobi declaration on unity.[3]

Even this very brief sketch of the course to date of the conciliar process for JPIC reveals its essentially ecodomical character. That is, the quest for conciliar agreements or covenants is concerned with establishing binding ways of living in ecodomical union. This means that JPIC is an ecodomical formula defining the substance of the process.

What is at stake here is not just an ecumenical programme but the very nature of the church. The immensity of the task also reflects the spiritual need involved. That "Come, Holy Spirit — renew the whole creation", the theme of the Canberra assembly, reflects the ancient Christian cry, *Veni, Creator Spiritus*, is of profound spiritual significance.

Common work for a truthful image of reality

At Seoul some 400 delegates from the member churches of the WCC, together with representatives of other major religions and experts, set themselves the task of producing a document that would:

— offer an exact and comprehensible picture of a reality marked by injustice, lack of peace and destruction of nature;

— state the challenges to Christian faith posed by this reality and formulate them as "affirmations";

— make resolutions and establish a binding form of action in three exemplary problematical areas (at Seoul a fourth was added).

This plan failed. Not enough consideration was given to the very different ways in which the delegates interpreted the problems involved. One could summarize the difficulties by saying that at Seoul the experiences of everyday death confronted the fears of possible death. Anyone who sees children dying of starvation every day will not be particularly shocked at the prospect of possible deaths as a result of global warming in the year 2030. Those worried about the possibility of millions of deaths in a nuclear war will merely shake their heads, even if with some understanding, at the martial enthusiasm of a national resistance fighter, who will in turn tend to dismiss the scenario of a nuclear winter as abstract and improbable. Those whose research has provoked fears of the worst possible climatic disasters facing the next generation may deplore the injustice of sex tourism but may not find it quite so world-shakingly important as others do.

The delegates' different agendas and varying experiences necessarily had a blocking effect at Seoul which could not be dispelled by a few days' discussion. Many of the participants asserted the priority of their own perceptions of world problems. Under pressure from a large number of delegates, the question of racism was introduced as a fourth exemplary field of action for covenanting — in addition to a just economic order, a demilitarized concept of mutual security and protection of the earth's integrity. Some insisted that justice was more important than peace or preservation of the creation. Others put peace first; others the safeguarding of creation.

The excessive emotional pressure resulting from the unbearable degree of complexity that we have mentioned earlier was also apparent at Seoul. Accounts of present and future misery were so abundant that they tended to drive people instinctively back to their own established patterns of analysis.

In fact, months and not days of intensive exchange of experiences, information and impressions would have been needed to arrive at common declarations. Even if it had been possible, the "conciliar process" would still have to be seen as a learning process, so that a worldwide convocation would not in any case pronounce a final word but only formulate observations in a way that would stimulate rethinking in the churches.

It would have been more fruitful to conceive of the Seoul texts as an initial attempt to orient discussion in the member churches, which could have been followed at the Canberra assembly by an agreement to produce regular "state of the earth" reports. The resources for these would include the case studies and reference materials available in United Nations documentation and the annual reports of scientific institutes. The aim would be not just to offer general analyses but to use selected case histories to elucidate the actual connections between local injustice and global destruction, between negligence today and its consequences in the next generation. The goal must be to understand justice, peace and integrity of creation as three interlocking dimensions of each specific situation, comprising a "perichoretic" formula that is meaningful only as long as each dimension is understood and interpreted in terms of the other two. Just as life within the Trinity is perichoretic, so, too, is life in the creation of the triune God; and all learning and working in and between the churches must therefore be perichoretic too.

Consequently, I propose that justice, peace and integrity of creation should be seen as expressing the ecodomical vocation of Christians. Since the political, scientific, economic and ecological components of life are constantly changing, our view of things can approximate reality only if we try over and again to see this network of aspects in new ways. This is impossible for individuals or local groups. Only a universal community of churches, which is most comprehensively represented in the World Council of Churches, can perform this service to truth.

A second ground for such regular "state of the earth" reports is that we need communal efforts at the global level if we are to hope to counter internationally operative systems of lies, deception and confusion.

Telling the truth means calling things by name. It implies unmasking the linguistic confusion and deceptions of military interests and the intentionally euphemistic or technically misleading terminology used for weapons of mass destruction and for scenarios of nuclear or "conventional" warfare. Both the element of self-deception and the intention to deceive the public must be revealed. This also applies to industrial management and to politics.

We referred earlier to the manipulation of the media during the Gulf War as evidence of how readily journalists can come to surrender the right to free expression of opinion once fought for so fiercely. A concern for truthful images of reality also includes a struggle for free and accurate information and thus for human rights and democratic structures. If reality is accessible only by telling the truth, then we cannot allow ourselves to become accustomed to the constant deceptions of advertising. There can be no apathetic acceptance of or false peace with the soap-opera industry or the glorification of violence in the media. We must be especially aware of the dislocating effect of the media on children and young people.

The struggle to obtain truthful accounts of reality is an ongoing battle against deliberate attempts to confuse human beings. Telling the truth also means resisting lies. For that, worldwide co-operation is needed among agencies active in media criticism — a new global network of "lie-detectors" to inculcate critical resistance, protect regional variety, stabilize the self-reliance of nations and peoples and, above all, educate the minds and consciences of the next generation to distinguish truth from lies. Such an effort cannot of course stop at the boundaries of the churches. All over the world Christians live with other people of different beliefs who are nevertheless intensively involved in the fight for truth.

Ecodomical union seeks truth and wisdom in all human beings, because it is intent on acknowledging the one *pneuma* of truth in all of them. But it will perish if it does not include the dimension of endurance. Without steadfast preparedness for risk and persecution, the concern for justice, peace and integrity of creation cannot succeed. This concern also demands a great degree of solidarity, which is evident when we look at a further aspect of working for truth.

Overcoming discrepancies between wishes and needs

If we wish to undertake work in ecodomical covenant in the light of truth, we must be concerned with the truth about ourselves as partners in ecodomical union. We must deal not only with different experiences and circumstances but also with differences in mentality and cultural formation. There are other deep-seated tensions and conflicts which are seldom voiced. We shall now turn to some of these that affect people from the first and third worlds.

Even among Christians from poor countries bitter feelings about their rich "brothers and sisters" are growing. We have to take this very seriously. Above all, financial dependence constantly evokes deep resentment. People in the third world are obliged to accept unsuitable "project criteria" to satisfy inspectors and accountants who often have no understanding of how the money is to be used — and even to express gratitude to them.

The psychological tension arising from such dependency situations hinders work in ecodomical union. This was evident again and again during the Seoul convocation. For instance, when a US scientist warns against building more atomic bombs, it is difficult to avoid the suspicion that he is arguing thus merely to support the nuclear superiority of his own country. Again, when climate experts speak of the dire consequences of automobile traffic, we have to imagine the effect of that warning on those for whom the freedom associated with owning their own car is no more than a lifelong dream.

This kind of resentment is not unjustified. There are action groups in the first world who have abandoned their engagement in the intractable problems of the third world in order to devote themselves to environmental questions. There are New Age groups that wax eloquent about the "harmony of the cosmos" without any intention of altering their own life-style or engaging in a radical critique of the dominant world economic system.

Moreover, almost all representatives of the rich churches suffer from guilt feelings. They know that they are implicated in an unjust system. They are plagued by their sense of complicity in that system and troubled by their powerlessness to change it. At ecumenical meetings or during visits to partner churches in the third world they are seen only as a potential source of financial support for this or that urgent project.

This inner division sometimes leads them to adopt the theological vocabulary of the third world (for example, liberation theology) or to favour "African" dancing and singing in their worship. Obviously, there is something very artificial about "solidarity" that goes no further than this.

Some representatives of rich churches understand quite well the criticism of the ways of the established churches but cannot go so far as to accept a radical jettisoning of existing patterns. They take seriously the argument that, for instance, to get rid of the church taxes in Germany would not only endanger hundreds of thousands of jobs but also have a devastating effect on many life-saving projects in the third world.

In addition, there are many committed men and women in the rich world of the north who in fact live frugally and even abstemiously. When they travel to impoverished regions, they are annoyed to discover some "representatives" of the poor living far from frugally or exhibiting towards those beneath them on the social or economic scale attitudes that have long since — and quite rightly — been discarded at home.

All this raises the problem of the contradictions between our wishes and our life-projects.

Concern with justice, peace and the integrity of the creation leads inevitably to a critical discussion of our consumer behaviour and life-style. For Christians in the societies of excessive consumption there is only one conclusion: "Consume less! Recycle more!" But what happens when they propose such things in ecumenical gatherings? Often they find little response and become disillusioned. What they must realize is that their quest for being satisfied with sufficiency comes from an actual experience of having more than enough while the people sitting opposite them have always been forced to live with what barely suffices. Experiences of constant need and wretchedness can also evoke an insatiable desire for things.

Is plenty a precondition of contentedness? Did Christ not come from the fullness of God before emptying himself to the point of death on the cross (Phil. 2:5-11)? Evidently *pleroma* and *kenosis*, plenty and self-emptying, go together.

There is no straight road from forced impoverishment to voluntary poverty. Just as rich people can be voracious for and addicted to things, so people who live in wretched conditions can greedily crave possessions. It is important for ecumenical understanding to accept these contradictions in life-projects. Living the good and simple life is not a matter of merely discovering the median between too much and too little. The good and worthy life implies a conversion, which is far from self-evident either for rich people or for those who live in misery.

It is my impression that there is not enough discussion and exchange of ideas about contradictory life-projects in ecumenical assemblies. These polarities remain present as uncomprehended irritation and anger, serving to increase feelings of mistrust, suspicion and offence. Such problems are not aired openly in worship but are covered over with conciliatory songs, words and gestures.

It is precisely worship that has the task of setting before God these processes in which we become involuntarily and reciprocally guilty — which means exposing them to the light of truth. It is in worship that we repeat the prayer Jesus taught: "Forgive us our debts, *as we also have forgiven our debtors.*" Unfortunately, the forgiveness of sins, which plays a central role in Christian creeds as the work of the Holy Spirit, has thus far remained something rather alien to the ecumenical movement.

Concern with historical guilt

This syndrome of resentment, acrimony and division arising from the profound economic, political and cultural polarities of our time has its historical antecedents. Behind today's bitterness lie yesterday's experiences of enslavement, degradation and extermination. And the invasions of Africa, America and Asia by European nations usually proceeded under the twin symbols of sword and cross.

The monstrous crime of the slave trade remains not only in the memories of the descendants of the slaves but in those of the children of the slave-owners. Something like that is ineradicable, even long after slavery has been officially prohibited. The burden of colonialism stays in the mind of every nation affected by it — all the more so because today's dominant world economic system maintains and even refines the old structures of dependence, as is evident from the debt crisis. Along with these memories, which play an inevitable role in ecumenical gatherings of "brothers and sisters", are the actual divisions between the churches, still unhealed, which provided the original impetus for the ecumenical movement itself.

The statement on unity by the Canberra assembly, mentioned earlier in this chapter, calls the divisions between the churches "scandalous" and "sinful", emphasizes the koinonia of the churches and speaks of "a common mission witnessing to the gospel of God's grace to all people and serving the whole of creation".[4] But if, as one post-Canberra commentator observed, the traditional confessional polarities have been thoroughly debated in the course of fifty years of ecumenism, how is it that these divisions remain unreconciled?[5] The fact is that this observation applies only to traditional discourse about the history of doctrine and systematic theology, which is only one aspect of the reasons for separation and division. From the perspectives of pastoral psychology and the history of culture, other much more painful divisions would be revealed: deep-seated prejudices, ethnic and cultural polarities, distorted images of the devotional and liturgical practice of other churches, condemnations of teachings, persecutions, discrimination, feelings of superiority, power-seeking, assertions of dominance. It is incorrect simply to bracket these realities as "non-theological factors", for they are elements that mark the identity and self-awareness of the churches at least as strongly as dogmatic convictions.

If people talk and behave as if these denominational and confessional "identities" are sacrosanct, they are really saying that the sensitive history of profound injuries should not be exposed, because it would mean bringing the deeply rooted history of reciprocal guilt into the daylight — which is something traditional ecumenical discourse does not tackle. This is not to suggest that nothing further should be done to expand the area of converging doctrinal conviction, such as the so-called Lima text on *Baptism, Eucharist and Ministry* from the WCC Faith and Order Commission. But such declarations cannot deal appropriately with the underlying guilt, which requires procedures of forgiveness and reconciliation.

There are in fact some historical precedents for such an admission of guilt, which have had exceptionally liberating results. One could point to the encounter between representatives of the Evangelical Church in Germany and the WCC-in-process-of-formation in Stuttgart in 1945, which did lead, as the participants hoped, to "a new beginning". Or one could mention the historic meeting in 1966 between the Ecumenical Patriarch Athenagoras and Pope Paul VI, when the anathemas of 1054 were lifted. The acknowledgment of war guilt by the United Church of Japan (Kyodan), and the Rustenberg Declaration of the white Dutch Reformed Church in South Africa, repenting of its support for apartheid, were both in line with this tendency. Whatever their limitations, these confessions of guilt created a space for forgiveness and for imaginative and trusting co-operation.

But these remain exceptions. The recognition that the ecumenical movement must be a movement of forgiveness if it is to lead to authentic koinonia has not yet been expressed in a sufficiently enthusiastic and practical way. Thus the development of ecumenism seems to get arrested at the point of maintaining good-neighbourly relations — a clear improvement over the religious wars of times past but far short of the real goal of the unity of the churches. That goal cannot rest content with the status quo, but demands further moves that include overcoming the history of guilt which remains a barrier between many churches.

For this we need not more "doctrinal conversations" but new forms of encounter and exchange, liturgical rites and joint practical action that will allow us to express and work through the pain of past injustice.

Working for the truth cannot succeed without working through historical guilt. As long as we are affected by our guilt, by acrimony and shame and by injuries and anger, we shall be unable to rejoice in our diversities.

The Canberra unity statement refers to the scandal of separation but does not go on to raise the problem of the associated guilt. It declares that differences rooted in theological traditions and different cultural, ethnic or historical contexts are part of the nature of community, but does not criticize them from the viewpoint of creation theology. It mentions that the churches have to learn from one another how to join together in action for justice and peace and caring for God's creation, but nowhere indicates how the structural changes necessary for that might be brought about.

A clearer approach to this question comes from the report of the section of the Canberra assembly which treated the subtheme "Holy Spirit — Transform and Sanctify Us!":

Churches have anathematized each other, and have contributed to polarization leading some to define themselves in opposition to others. The churches need to repent of their stances and actions in respect to each other, and to take responsibility for the positions which they adopt and for their theologies. Without *repentance and forgiveness* no new creation as reconciled communities can emerge...[6]

These words point to a direction in which ecumenical fellowship can be deepened. Without such a penitential remembrance of the guilty past there can be no common work in ecodomical union. The goal of ecodomical union is necessarily a mission of love that seeks to promote the protection, welfare and salvation of all that lives. Therefore the diversity of the churches has to prove itself in the diverse forms of service they provide locally and regionally. The various denominations must ask themselves what are their own special charisms that can be called into service to creation. What specific contributions can they make and how much independence do they need to do so?

It is not a matter of dissolving the various denominations into a uniform and diffuse "united church". The goal must be to deploy the strengths of individual denominations and confessions in the advancement and construction of local ecodomical centres, and to make their organizational independence and individuality — or "identity" — flexible and available.

The truth throws light on the tasks that face Christianity in ecodomical union, and brings all participants and their history under the spotlight, the clear and steady illumination of the Spirit. The truth makes clear what is to be done and enlightens us about the burdens of guilt that weigh down the community of the churches. The truth about the world is bound up with the truth about ourselves. It is indivisible.

NOTES

[1] D. M. Paton, ed., *Breaking Barriers: Nairobi 1975*, Geneva, 1976, p.60.
[2] The report is found in *Peace with Justice*, Geneva, Conference of European Churches, 1989.
[3] Cf. Michael Kinnamon, ed., *Signs of the Spirit*, Geneva, 1991, pp.172ff.
[4] *Ibid.*, p.173.
[5] Cf. R. Frieling, *Ökumenische Akzente: Eindrücke und Erkenntnisse aus Canberra*, Frankfurt, 1991, p.59.
[6] Kinnamon, *op. cit.*, p.115 (italics added).

Chapter 20

The Reality of Solidarity
in the Ecodomical Covenant

Truth can be a terrible thing, especially when it throws its light on the terror of injustice and vanity, the horror of cruelty and violence, not only around us but also — what is worse — inside us. Truth blocks our escapes into ideological simplifications and dismantles our mechanisms of evasion, deception and self-justification.

Where do we get the strength to cope with truth? We are not heroes; we need ecodomical help for ourselves. We need consolation and solidarity; we long for friends who share our anguish. Life in the ecodomical covenant is rooted in truth; but its life-sustaining springs lie in the *pneuma* of consolation and solidarity.

Struggling for forgiveness

When the ancient Christian creeds speak of the Holy Spirit, they proceed almost immediately to talk of the forgiveness of sins. Obviously our mothers and fathers in the faith knew that forgiveness is the way in which the power of the *pneuma* makes itself felt in people's lives. Yet today the idea of "forgiveness of sins" seems to have fallen into disrepute. Forgiveness and pardon have become cheap words, reminding us of what Dietrich Bonhoeffer said about "cheap grace".

Thus it is necessary to take a fresh look at the meaning of forgiveness. Under the heading of truth we had to confront the disturbing fact of guilt, so under the rubric of solidarity we need to explore what forgiveness is and how it works.

The process of forgiveness usually begins when someone faces his or her guilt about an unjust act done to another person. Without such awareness of guilt, there will be no room or opportunity for forgiveness. But to become conscious of guilt is to begin to feel its heavy burden, and that provokes the desire to ask the person wronged for forgiveness.

This request is difficult to make because it involves lowering oneself. In asking forgiveness, I make myself dependent on and even vulnerable to my "victim". I surrender the position of power that I wrongly assumed as a result of my injustice, for my injustice consisted of making myself more powerful and the other person less powerful than we really are. By asking to be forgiven I give up the superiority that I have "stolen" from the other.

As the guilty party, I can only ask for forgiveness, never demand it. Forgiveness can come only from the victim or from those entitled to speak on the victim's behalf. When people who have suffered an injustice forgive the perpetrator, they throw off the bonds of humiliation and regain the space needed to act freely and the worth and power that were "stolen" from them.

When we grant forgiveness, we have to live through a moment of deep pain, because we are made newly aware of the original injustice and, as it were, relive its horror. Many people are afraid of forgiving precisely because they do not want to return to the place of their hurt. On the other hand, those who ask for forgiveness also have to experience the bitter moment in which they see their injustice for what it really is, and feel the ignominy of shame. Many people shy away from asking forgiveness because they do not want to return to the place of their shame. So the act of forgiving is a moment of disarming truth for both sides. As they give up their façades, the arsenals of accusation and defence become superfluous. As both sides exchange their bitter memories, they liberate each other from the chains of guilt and anger, of hurt and shame.

Hannah Arendt remarks that forgiveness constantly occurs in our everyday private life. Without forgiveness it would be impossible for us to deal freely with one another. She describes forgiveness as the contingent and creative power that enables us to break though the chain of inevitability that would otherwise bind us forever to former injustice:

> Forgiving can never be predicted; it is the only reaction that acts in an unexpected way and thus retains, though being a reaction, something of the original character of action. Forgiving... is the only reaction which does not merely react but acts anew and unexpectedly, unconditioned by the act which provoked it and therefore freeing from its consequences both the one who forgives and the one who is forgiven.[1]

But if forgiveness means liberation from the cruel chains of former injustice, why do we find it so difficult to ask for and to grant forgiveness? It is the encounter with pain and the realization of our vulnerability that make us fearful of engaging in an act which, deep in our hearts, we are longing for.

Arendt believes that the power of forgiveness came into the world with Jesus. "The discoverer of the role of forgiveness in the realm of human affairs was Jesus of Nazareth,"[2] she says, citing several texts in the gospel, especially the well-known petition in the Lord's Prayer: "Forgive us our debts, as we also have forgiven our debtors."

I think this view is only partly correct. Certainly Jesus' behaviour up to his death on the cross was marked by an extraordinary freedom, by a lack of prejudice that allowed him to approach even the most "impossible" people without any ill-feeling. Jesus lived in the power of forgiveness because he was God's Spirit in person. But if it were indeed true that the possibility of forgiveness was first manifested in human history in the person of Jesus Christ, there would have been no such thing as forgiveness before then and no forgiveness outside Jesus' sphere of influence. Clearly that is not the case. Instead we should see forgiveness as a *pneumatic* reality, which thus can and does appear in all human societies.

The essential point, it seems to me, is that the process of forgiveness requires the element of contingency that enables us to find the formula — the gesture or the words — of release. Forgiveness is a process between two people or groups of people. But a third factor is also involved: the initiatory impulse, the moment of courage that opens our mouths, the tiny wavering flame of trust which allows us to believe that the person of whom we ask forgiveness is ready to forgive. Without this trust we would not dare disarm ourselves.

This factor of contingency, theologically speaking an expression of *pneuma*, is not something to which only Christians have access. It may be expressed in friendship, as when a mutual friend brings together two people who have been alienated from each other, or in the mediation of social or political conflicts.

Anyone who has experienced forgiveness knows its liberating power. The burden of guilt and the weight of grievance are lifted. This does not mean that all injustice is simply forgotten, but much of the pain can be left behind in the sense that it loses its peculiar power to hurt; and when a process of forgiveness is truly complete, the injustice itself is really done away with.

But there is also injustice of such overwhelming gravity that neither the guilty nor the victims *wish* to forget it. This does not mean that they want to reproach one another for it all over again — for then it would not really be forgiven — but that they want to bring it as a common painful memory before the forum of conscience, so that something of this kind will never be repeated. This is why the Holocaust of the Jewish people by the Nazis must be remembered, as a common commitment to preventing such atrocities from happening again.

This is a decisive point. Forgiveness means a break with the burdensome past, a new beginning and a radically changed way of behaving. That does not exclude the possibility of our reverting to our old, guilty ways and once again needing to be forgiven. Essentially, however, forgiveness marks the beginning of a new common relationship and thus of a new community in which tasks can be undertaken jointly.

Therefore, forgiveness is a central element of consolation, not only because it can heal the mental and psychological pains and poisonous consequences of guilt and offence, but also because it establishes a new solidarity. Forgiveness releases mutual trust and this serves as the cornerstone for constructive cooperation.

Before developing this further, we should briefly take up three objections:

1. The forgiveness of sins is entirely a matter of our relationship to God. Only God can forgive.

This objection overlooks the fact that every sin of which we are guilty before God is also committed against our own created dignity, against other people or against nature. Similarly, there is no wrong done to ourselves, other people or other forms of life that does not make us guilty also in the sight of God the Creator. Guilt must be understood both vertically and horizontally.

It is certainly true that we human beings continually sin against one another and against God and therefore need forgiveness as continuously as we need air to breathe. Nevertheless, forgiveness is not an automatic thing that changes nothing. Every instance of forgiveness worthy of the name is a break that opens up new possibilities.

Forgiveness occurs through the power of the *pneuma* between people and communities. Forgiveness emanates from God and simultaneously from others. It enables another spirit to replace the spirit of vengeance and hatred, namely, the Spirit of Jesus Christ, who prayed from the cross for those who persecuted him. So hatred is replaced by reconciliation, deception is rewarded with honesty, mistrust gives way to frank cooperation.

On the other hand, it needs to be maintained that in the strict sense, there is no such thing as restitution. Making reparations does not liberate us from the burdens of the past. Guilt cannot be "repaired" or "repaid". By its very nature, it is unique. No suffering can be undone by means of something else, be it new suffering or financial reparations.

But forgiveness is an unconditional act that breaks the chains with the past. It is an act of liberation which at the same time initiates a radically new communal practice. Obviously this will include material and financial compensations to correct the damages as far as possible. But the goal is to start new and creative forms of living and working together that can replace old polarities and enmities.

2. There is no such thing as forgiveness between communities, institutions and peoples.

The second objection is that forgiveness is an exclusively personal category. In this view, it can occur between marriage partners, between parents and children, between colleagues and friends, but not between opposed social groups, between churches and above all between nations.

But this argument is mistaken. It is not only as individual persons that we are subjects of our behaviour, but also as members of groups and nations, just as we experience ourselves as objects and victims of injustice and crime not only as individuals but in communities. In the succession of generations we are dependent on others who became guilty or who suffered injustice before we existed. Whether they like it or not, German people who were born long after the second world war find themselves linked to the atrocities of the Nazi period; and the trauma of occupation by the German armies lingers on in subsequent generations in many countries of Europe. Everywhere in the world, the history of nations is tied up with memories of guilt and shame.

These collective memories are deeply shaped by the injustices people have committed or suffered. They remain alive in songs, sagas and dances, in monuments, rites and ceremonies, thus exerting a profound though often unconscious effect on our communal and political activity.

But if we cannot avoid speaking of collective guilt and trauma, surely it is warranted to ask what collective forgiveness looks like. An example of this quest can be seen in the setting up of national reconciliation commissions in the Esquipulas peace process in Central America, initiated by Nobel Peace Prize laureate Oscar Arias in 1989. The task of these commissions was to resolve social conflicts in the participating countries. The term "reconciliation" obviously has certain religious connotations, underlined in practice by the fact that most of these commissions were chaired by Catholic bishops. But these committees were unable to bring about the desired reconciliation. Why?

The issue of "reconciliation" was discussed while the historical reality of guilt was avoided. The dominant class of landowners and people with power, who bore the guilt for the unjust systems which provoked civil wars and social strife, never acknowledged their need for reconciliation. To this day there has been no public admission of guilt from the *latifundistas*, the military establishment or the leaders of the infamous death squads. And as long as the ruling powers insist on "business as usual", there can be no new beginning. Without some form of repentance all efforts at reconciliation remain null and void.

Yet this example does not prove that there can be no such thing as forgiveness between nations or between various groups within society. According to Hannah Arendt, forgiveness as a reality has not yet found any place in political practice.[3] But this is not entirely true.

For example, Brian Frost cites many instances where forgiveness has played a part in political affairs.[4] The beginnings are there, but consistent imagination is required to design forms of forgiveness that are politically feasible. In Zimbabwe, for example, the attempt to bring together the parties to the civil war after long years of embittered conflict met with considerable success. In Namibia, too, the National Council of Churches played a major role in resolving the problem of heavy burdens of guilt resulting from conflict.

3. Forgiveness allows injustice to go unpunished.

Any talk of forgiveness provokes immediate suspicions of a cover-up. It is clear that forgiveness cannot replace justice. An easy amnesty for war criminals can only deepen the bitterness and hatred in the people who have suffered. But where is the line to be drawn between those offences which are brought to court and those which are not? Even if it were conceivable that courts could exercise justice comprehensively, forgiveness as liberation from the chains of former grievances and offences would still be necessary. Whereas justice must strive to provide and ensure equal options for all members of a nation or people, forgiveness has to do with the *healing of memories*. Therefore it must be made into a constructive aspect of the establishment of reliable and trustworthy relations between people, groups and nations. We cannot speak of ecodomy as long as there are no processes available for freeing ourselves from the mutilating effects of historical guilt.

These reflections lead to the question of forgiveness between churches. It is widely accepted that it is the churches' joint responsibility to work for justice and peace and exercise a healing and saving ministry in the world. Yet they are themselves caught up in a long history of divisions, prejudices and suspicions.

Over the past several decades, an impressive series of commissions has produced numerous studies that are helping the churches to know one another better. These dialogues have clearly revealed many common aspects. But we also know the traumatic grievances and resentments that lie hidden beneath the friendly relations among church officials. The time has come to take a decisive step and look for genuine expressions of forgiveness. This cannot be brought about by academic study groups but requires representative symbolic expression. In other words, the churches need new rituals of forgiveness. Their aim should be to heal the hurting memories, not necessarily to arrive at unification schemes. A process of liberation from the sting of past grievances would probably open up a wide array of joint actions in such areas as education, diakonia and media work. Such rituals would have to become part of the churches' annual festivals in order to ensure that forgiveness becomes a part of the joint and living memory of reconciliation in the life of churches and communities.

Only when the chain of condemnations, prejudices and ill feelings is broken by authentic rituals of healing will it be possible to celebrate the eucharist together and to open up the way towards genuine ecodomical communities which help the world to see that the Spirit of love is indeed alive.

Healing the wounds of the nations

The churches are not the only organizations torn apart by memories of unresolved conflicts, of course. The relationships of ethnic groups and nations are overshadowed by memories of bloody wars and massacres, periods of oppression and near annihilation. Three examples may elucidate what I have in mind.

1. At an ecumenical conference in Accra in 1974, Bishop Lesslie Newbigin visited Elmira Castle, the centre of the slave trade on the Ghana coast. To his horror, he discovered that the chapel stood directly above the place where the captive Africans were chained before being shipped to America. A hole in the chapel floor allowed them to be observed during services, so that the worshippers could be sure that everything was "in order" below. Newbigin comments:

> I am always amazed that these crimes can be so easily forgotten. Ever since that visit I have wished that some representative Englishman — an Archbishop or Prime Minister — might come to Ghana and go down into that dungeon, kneel down on the floor and offer a prayer of contrition. I still hope it may happen.[5]

2. During a 1988 conference in Bad Segeberg, Germany, on the theme "Reconciliation with the Peoples of the Soviet Union", Nikolai Portugalev, then Mikhail Gorbachev's advisor on German affairs, spoke of the terrible suffering and devastation caused in his homeland by the German forces during the second world war. He referred to the reconciliation between the Polish and German peoples and to Chancellor Willy Brandt's kneeling in repentance before the monument erected in Warsaw in memory of the Jews murdered by the Germans. Then he said: "I do not think of reconciliation in terms of reparations; for that is over and nobody thinks of that any longer. Instead, what we people in the Soviet Union are hoping for is an act of kneeling down — not in the literal sense, of course, but one which comes from the heart of the German people."[6]

3. Former Zambian president Kenneth Kaunda has written of forgiveness as having a political dimension. Speaking as a representative of suppressed and colonialized peoples, he remarks that forgiveness is not a single act but a continual willingness "to live in a new day without looking back and ransacking the memory for occasions of bitterness and resentment".[7] Of course, Kaunda is aware that forgiveness is no substitute for justice, but

he also knows that justice without forgiveness will not enable us to emerge from the shadow of injustice. He writes: "To claim forgiveness while perpetuating injustice is to live a fiction; to fight for justice without also being prepared to offer forgiveness is to render your struggle null and void."[8] The words of this African leader enable us to see that forgiveness has the power to break the mental chains that lock us to feelings of resentment and revenge and to liberate us from repeating the injustices we are trying to combat.

Kaunda also knows that there are injustices of such monstrous proportions that there is just no way to compensate for them. The world does not have enough money, he maintains, to "make good" for the death of six million Jews. He goes on to say:

> I have seen the bodies of innocent refugees in Zambia, blown to bits by Rhodesian bombers, and my soul has been so tormented by my raging mind and angry heart that had I not been able to forgive my enemies because Christ has forgiven me, I should have become deranged with fury.[9]

Kaunda's confession clarifies that forgiveness entails a twofold liberation because it frees both the guilty and the victims. Forgiveness is not a special virtue but the fruit of the insight that in the last resort every human being needs to be forgiven. Thus forgiveness is a fruit of unrelenting self-awareness.

These three diverse people — a British theologian, a Soviet Communist and an African politician — testify to the degree to which the daily life of peoples is marked by memories of collective injustice. Newbigin and Portugalev express the desire that the descendants of the nations that have accumulated massive guilt should be willing to fall to their knees in acknowledgment of it. Here, falling to one's knees is considered as a representative symbolic act of repentance and voluntary humiliation that might restore the dignity of humiliated peoples.

Since politicians, ever preoccupied with maintaining their power, will usually lack the courage for such a symbolic act of humility, it is perhaps up to the churches, who should know something of the liberating power of forgiveness, to take the lead here. And if these churches had overcome the historical guilt between themselves and other churches, they would possess the spiritual authority to engage themselves for the forgiveness of the guilt that burdens their peoples.

It is said that "time heals all wounds". But the best that time can do for the wounds of guilt and offence is something like habituation, which can seem akin to normality as long as no new crisis is reopening the old wounds. Two examples come to mind from recent European history. When divided Germany was re-united after the fall of the Berlin Wall, considerable alarm was raised among its neighbours because harsh memories of two world wars were reawakened. In the former Yugoslavia, ancient and unforgiven ethnic conflicts have surfaced again and are caus-ing abominable cruelties. Nothing is healed that is not forgiven. The same is true elsewhere in the world. Time cannot heal the memories of the inconceivable sufferings endured by colonialized and enslaved peoples, nor does it heal memories of shame in the descendants of former colonial masters and slave-owners.

Here the ecumenical movement has the task of facing up not only to the history of guilt between the churches but also to the guilt of their nations, through acts of representative and vicarious political diakonia. The beginnings are there. In reference to Portugalev's remarks cited earlier, it should be noted that the German churches played an important role in initiating the heal-ing of relations between the German and Polish peoples. Without this work the *Ostpolitik* of Willy Brandt would not have been possible. With regard to the peoples of what was then the Soviet Union, church representatives have requested forgiveness on sev-eral occasions, and the Russian Orthodox Church offered forgive-ness very soon after the second world war. Yet the churches have not yet succeeded in bringing about an official representative and symbolic act of forgiveness between their nations.

Recalling Bishop Newbigin's hope, what would happen if representatives of the Council of Churches for Britain and Ire-land, along with the Archbishop of Canterbury, were to assemble together with representatives of the All Africa Conference of Churches in Elmira Castle on the Ghana coast, where the descen-dants of the "masters" would plead for forgiveness and the descendants of the enslaved nations would offer freedom? Would such an unprecedented act not enable them to work together more freely and with fewer prejudices than before?

When Christian churches begin to regard each other as part-ners in an ecodomical covenant they will discover that there is a public ministry of consolation and solidarity. It cannot solve all the problems, of course, but it can help people to begin travelling the road of disarming confidence which will lead to unexpected peace.

Networks of friends

The large-scale problems we have just been discussing should not obscure our attention to everyday difficulties that can be severe vexations to our spirit. I am referring to the permanent misunderstandings, the opposition of goals and desires, the suspicions and humiliations that result from our torn and unjust world. These burdens play their oppressive part even within churches, not only in their international relations but also within local communities. I am thinking of third world support groups that cannot cope with the growing impoverishment in the countries they "care for", or with their own lack of success, and therefore collapse. There are other issue-groups that fail under the pressure of the ongoing struggle and its increasing complexity. There are scientists whose research work has given them a clear picture of future disasters but who cannot get a hearing among their fellow experts, or even among friends in their own church community.

How can we ward off the danger of "numbing", of psychological capitulation and emotional impoverishment?

We need people who understand us, groups and communities in which our complaints and anxieties can be heard and our anger and frustration are understood. We need consoling communities, places of reliable solidarity.

The traditional parochial system is not able to respond well to the multi-faceted relationships of modern societies. Nor is it capable of meeting all the pastoral and spiritual demands of many people. Unfortunately, many congregations are on the verge of turning into "life-style enclaves",[10] groups which develop their own specific forms of communication and conduct. Often the "core parish" is such an enclave, which tends to treat as "external" everything that does not fit into its system of thought and is quickly denounced as having to do with "politics" or "economics" or "ecology". Such activities are dismissed as foreign to the "central mission" of the church. Like every life-style enclave, such introverted parishes try to keep to themselves in their trusted space and seek to maintain them undisturbed. New worshippers often feel that they are unwanted intruders, and socially and politically committed groups are pushed to the periphery. Consequently, many "secular" groups concerned with human rights or ecological questions see "church" as something hiding away in a pious cocoon, irrelevant to social tasks.

So it is not surprising that committed groups should get together outside traditional parish communities. This explains much of the attractiveness of charismatic renewal movements or, in Latin America, the wide distribution of Christian base communities.

Of course, these groups, in their turn, composed of active and like-minded people, can also easily become life-style enclaves. Christian parishes and communities have to be on their guard against this tendency and to resist it with determination. They will succeed in doing so if they are ecodomical centres functioning under the enlivening energy of *pneuma*. If the dominant atmosphere is one of joy, trust and kindness, we willingly open up in readiness for new tasks. Isolation, insecurity and marginalization fade when we try to help one another constructively.

In the mid-1980s, the South Africa group in a parish in Geneva held a series of critical evening discussions on the role of banks in South Africa. One of the participants was a church elder and a leading official in a Geneva bank. At the end of the series he told the others that if everything that had been said was true he would have to resign his job. The others did not know what to say. Shortly afterwards he did in fact resign — not from his position in the bank but as an elder. He turned his back on the parish, bought and renovated an old farmhouse outside the city and now spends all his weekends there with his family.

The South Africa group had opened the banker's eyes but could not see him through the consequences of this decision. Perhaps the group should have told him that for a year they would make good the loss in his salary and help him to find new work. They would be a community of friends to him and his family. Perhaps, they could have said, his decision would encourage other bankers suffering from the amorality of their business to do something similar.

Solidarity is not just a matter of words. It is a shaping principle of ecodomical centres. Anyone who is uprooted by an encounter with truth — and every conversion is a kind of uprooting — finds his or her feet on firm ground again if the community is able to provide real comfort.

I once visited an independent church in a poor quarter of Accra, Ghana, and found that the parish was divided into groups of friends. Many members of these groups had left the country-side and had no social and family connections in the city. Available for their members in all their life-crises, these groups of friends became responsible for caring, for making their members feel at home and for emotional stabilization. This seems to characterize many African congregations, whose internal arrangements constitute something like a "para-family" structure to care for their members. It is not surprising to discover that women play a leading role in these internal groups. In many cases, the decisive problem is not material need; rather, it is emotional isolation, loss of meaning and other forms of psychological stress that awaken the consoling power of the parish.

Christian parishes should be seen as communities of consolation and solidarity. In many cases it will be necessary to form something like neighbourhood groups within parishes to care for lonely elderly people or to help families with differently abled children. In other cases urban parishes may have to get together to deal with political, social or ecological concerns in more appropriate groupings. For instance, "ecological councils" could be formed in which environmental groups would work together with schools, city council representatives and state authorities. Another idea would be to form "ethical round tables", bringing together scientists and engineers with political and economic experts to exchange experiences as well as express their frustrations and anxieties.

On a regional level, "networks" have been formed, for example in the Evangelical Church in Baden, Germany. Another interesting initiative, also in Germany, is the ecumenical Pentecost celebration held every second year since 1983 in the North Elbian Lutheran Church. These assemblies bring specific issue-groups together with more traditional parish members in order to create a better awareness of each other and to prevent alienation and frustration. Significantly, these meetings take place during the Pentecost weekend, and the eucharistic celebration of God's Spirit at the centre gives new determination and hope to the people involved. Another very important initiative is the Kairos Movement, which coordinates political and economic issue-groups all over Europe.

It may well be that these "councils" and "initiatives" are still much too formal. In any case they run the risk of institutionalization if there is no real evidence of solidarity and therefore of friendship — a central dimension of the Christian faith.

The essence of consolation and solidarity is expressed in committed friendship. What friendship within the parish and friendship for the world can achieve is evident in the Society of Friends. But one does not have to become a Quaker in order to experience the comforting power of friendship. It is an essential Christian task to seek to establish friendship and to nurture it, so that the joys and grievances of our lives can be shared in unrestricted trust. When Christian parishes see themselves as networks of friendship, they will stand a good chance of overcoming the tendency to turn into life-style enclaves, as well as turning the world around them into a friendlier place.

The art of sharing burdens

"Bear one another's burdens, and in this way you will fulfil the law of Christ" (Gal. 6:2). This is an invitation to explore the imaginative strength of solidarity. Bearing another's burdens implies that human beings have their specific burdens but also that everyone has the capacity to help others with their problems. People certainly have loads of differing weight and complexity to bear and are troubled by them at different times. But there is more to it than that. When we try to help others with their burden, our own does not become heavier but lighter. It is as if bearing another's load releases a certain power that raises our own from our shoulders. This is the "law of Christ" which gives rest to all who "are weary and are carrying heavy burdens" (Matt. 11:28).

How does this relate to communities, parishes, groups and churches? Helping others to carry their loads is the mystery of consolation and solidarity. It turns into a burden, however, if we are left alone.

All churches have developed a closely woven fabric of burden-sharing, which is described by the Greek word *diakonia*. As international relations between the churches have developed and matured — for the most part through missionary relations and ecumenical organizations — ecumenical diakonia has also extended its influence. It has become a complex network of aid agencies and relief projects. In recent decades "development aid" has come into being, creating a veritable "aid industry".

But the impoverishment of two-thirds of the world is out-pacing any aid. Requests for solidarity and support come from every quarter. The structural injustice of the world economic system means that all aid measures drop into a bottomless pit and that aid organizations are unable to cope.

What can the churches do in this situation? Referring again to the World Council of Churches' initiative on Justice, Peace and the Integrity of Creation, we could say that churches and groups have many different ways of becoming involved, depending on their local conditions and socio-political means. Every form of involvement opens up various opportunities of learning, enrich-ment and correction. All genuine sharing is of a perichoretic nature. There is no giving without receiving, no teaching without learning.

This process is often called "networking". But that term is too technical. The following four considerations may give it more substance.

1. Coordination. Historical factors, including the work of missionary societies, traditional relationships dating back to the colonial era and specific trade associations have meant that certain areas of the world are much more closely interconnected than others.

More recent political, social and theological developments also come into play here. Consider, for example, the case of Nicaragua. When the Sandinista revolution triumphed, certain groups in Europe and North America became immensely enthusiastic about diaconal service and development under the new regime. Nicaragua's immediate neighbours, such as Guatemala or Belize, were no less urgently in need of aid. Yet they remained out of sight and out of mind because they were not "fashionable". Later, in 1990, when the Sandinistas were voted out of government, many overseas solidarity groups suddenly vanished from the Nicaraguan scene, even though the needs of the people were no less urgent.

Similarly, during the cold war, conservative circles in the West poured aid into some of the marginalized churches of Eastern Europe and the then-Soviet Union. Their support was sorely needed, but at the same time it served the interests of specific political groups behind the scenes.

One could cite many similar examples of unevenness and even trendiness in ecclesiastical solidarity campaigns. But aid has to be extended as justly and fairly as possible to all situations of need. Therefore, these initiatives must be more proficiently coordinated around the globe.

This is the context that gives the idea of a "conciliar process" practical meaning. Conciliar processes are needed to coordinate aid and to develop a structure of practical agreements and rules for practical cooperation. It would be a great achievement if the jungle of "established relations", with all its subtle power-games, were cleared in favour of a system of burden-sharing. Regular conciliar debates could help correct disparities and ensure fair, lasting and equitable relations between all partners.

It is necessary to begin working towards a worldwide burden-sharing system. The World Council of Churches should take the initiative in shaping such a conciliar process. To be sure, churches and aid agencies would be obliged to surrender some of their "independence". The process of coordination requires an approximate overview of existing relations and aid flows, so that we can discover which churches and regions are neglected. A clearing-house would be needed to provide information, to propose adjustments and emergency actions to the churches at the national and local levels.

2. Adjustment. Solidarity can never be static. Political and economic circumstances change so rapidly that partnerships and agreements must constantly be revised. Therefore, coordination has to be supplemented by correction and adjustment. In Europe, for example, the churches in the former Communist countries are faced with changing possibilities and tasks that were inconceivable only a few years ago. A conciliar process can deal with political and social changes of this kind and adapt the burden-sharing system accordingly. I would suggest that something like every six to seven years meetings should be held at all levels of the conciliar process in order to exchange experiences, discuss adjustments and re-determine where commitment is to be focused.

3. Unburdening. An often-overlooked aspect in our attempts to cope with need is that burden-sharing also includes unburdening. Pressures would be substantially reduced if a council or group of churches, in an African country for instance, knew who its partners were for a foreseeable period. The humiliating stress of constantly having to plead for finance for projects would then decrease. A trusting relationship would develop that could extend to parishes, communities, youth groups and other organizations. People at the grassroots could visit each other to reinforce the bonds of community. Genuine partnership would ease the disquieting feelings of belonging to the "have-nots" and having to beg for "help" all the time.

The element of unburdening can also be important for donor churches and groups. Very often the cries for help are heard by people who are already deeply committed. Confronted by an apparently endless stream of needs, they become frustrated. If, however, such parishes or groups were to commit themselves to a specific series of tasks within the framework of some ecumenically decided endeavour, they could concentrate on it with a clear conscience, assured that other communities and churches were aware of other important tasks and that a uniformly trustworthy network of relations would secure help for as many people in need as possible.

Precisely when people want to commit themselves and offer help, they should be sure that they can do it willingly and joyfully. In the long run, those who assume burdens because they think it is just a matter of doing their Christian duty will feel that they have taken on more than they can cope with and even become embittered.

4. Mutuality. Interchurch aid and development projects often produce a "one-way-mentality". Recipient groups and churches think they have nothing to offer in return. They are wrong. Are people in need of material assistance really unable to share? Do not the "rich" churches cry out for solidarity too? Everyone has something to give just as everyone needs to receive something. Prayers are as important as projects, and a song dedicated to a church group far away can be a source of great joy. Mutuality includes spiritual and material sharing. It is important also to underline the responsibility of those who receive aid for those who give. Where this is lacking, solidarity degenerates into mere alms-giving.

These four aspects of a worldwide system of burden-sharing combine material, ecclesiological and spiritual elements and give the conciliar process an ecodomically relevant and practical dimension. If that is the case, burden-sharing will be a comforting and inspiring experience. In the spirit of the Comforter, Christians and churches will become one another's "paracletic partners". As Philip Potter, the former general secretary of the World Council of Churches, has written:

> We are called to be Paracletes, to comfort and counsel one another. We are called to be beside each other, helping, exhorting, consoling, strengthening. This is what fellowship within our congregations and churches and between the churches around the world is all about.[11]

NOTES

[1] Hannah Arendt, *The Human Condition*, Chicago, 1958, p.241. On the problem of forgiveness from the perspective of pastoral psychology, see J. Patton, *Is Human Forgiveness Possible?*, Nashville, 1986.

[2] *Op. cit.*, p.238.

[3] *Ibid.*

[4] Brian Frost, *The Politics of Peace*, London, 1991.

[5] Quoted by Frost, *ibid.*, p.149.

[6] "Berichte und Analysen aus der Arbeit der Evangelischen Akademie Nordelbien", *Orientierung*, 1/1988, p.16.

[7] Quoted by Frost, *op. cit.*, pp.162f.

[8] *Ibid.*, p.163.

[9] *Ibid.*

[10] On this term see Robert Bellah et al., *Habits of the Heart: Individualism and Commitment in American Life*, New York, 1986, esp. pp.71ff.

[11] *Life in all its Fullness*, Geneva, 1981, p.33.

Chapter 21

The Ecodomical Covenant and the Power of Endurance

Making and keeping promises is the essence of every covenant, whether in marriage or between states. For the inner expression of this capacity we have used such terms as faithfulness, reliability and endurance. Instinctively, we react with distaste and even horror to lack of faithfulness and the breaking of agreements.

Hannah Arendt suggests two reasons why this is so: the "impossibility of foretelling the consequences of an act within a community of equals where everybody has the same capacity to act and thus relying upon the future" and the "darkness of the human heart, that is, the basic untrustworthiness of people who can never guarantee today who they will be tomorrow".[1] Both are essentially expressions of freedom.

The future contains the element of contingency; just as no one can foresee what nature holds in store, so, too, human beings are unfathomable, because they are free to act and because the consequences of their actions become all the more unpredictable as human interactions become increasingly complex.

Although this freedom may frighten us, we would not want to do without it, because we sense that it concerns the very core of our being. Therefore, totalitarian dictatorships and centrally planned economies are not viable in the long run, because they represent an inhuman attempt to manipulate the imponderability of the future and to get a hold on its fundamental contingency.

Nietzsche once described the human being as "the animal that may make promises". This capacity to make and keep promises is exactly the point at which human beings can deal with contingency and become masters of their freedom. When we promise one another to behave in a certain way, even if this demands certain sacrifices from us, then a ray of certainty can be glimpsed through the general fog of uncertainty. When we enter into a covenant with another, we mark out an area within which we can move with some security. The firmer the net of covenant, the greater our confidence.

The most profound expression of an assurance that trust-worthy forms of order are still available in the midst of chaos is to be found in the great myths of peoples. A familiar example comes from the book of Genesis. After the flood which signifies the return of chaos, God makes a covenant with Noah and with the earth: "As long as the earth endures, seedtime and harvest, cold and heat, summer and winter, day and night, shall not cease" (Gen. 8:22).

This covenant is made precisely because the human heart is untrustworthy and unreliable. That is why there must be some-thing like the great reliable rhythms of seedtime and harvest, and there must also be a covenant that enables trustworthiness to enter into unreliable human thought and action. Because nature is contingent, covenantal ordinances are needed to ensure the maintenance of day and night, summer and winter, cold and heat.

The covenant is established and enacted to ensure the contingent historicity of the creation and within it human freedom. In the perspective of the covenant the rhythms and laws of nature are designed to function not as automatic repetitive devices, but as reliable instances of order. This is the basis not only of the divine covenant but also of the human capacity to unite and to agree to think and act out of loyalty and faith.

What has been said earlier about ecodomy cannot be understood without the dimension of covenant and the possibility of endurance. If there were no such thing as the original trust in the reliability of the rhythms of nature, the confidence that what applies today will also apply tomorrow, who would have the courage to plan or project anything at all? All creative and constructive ecodomical processes must be undertaken in the secure knowledge that our past and present experiences can to some extent be extrapolated into the future — in other words, that time itself can be trusted.

But this raises the deepest problem of our age, when nuclear and ecological threats have indeed created the agonizing possibility of the end of time itself. When chaos can overwhelm the world at any moment, it becomes meaningless to remain faithful, to make and keep promises, to enter into covenants and to endure in them.

Under the destructive pressure of this doomsday-feeling, we must reaffirm the saving dimension of Christian eschatology.

The time to make the necessary changes seems to be running out. But the changes must be made in order to gain time. If we cannot gain time, we or our children might well be the "last human beings".

When time threatens to come to its end, we need time that opens up from across death. That is the point where eschatology and creation theology inform each other. The *rûah* who carries and creates the universe and the *rûah* who is incarnated in Jesus manifests her energies in the power of resurrection. The apocalyptic breathlessness of no-time is overcome. The resurrection of Jesus from the dead is the ultimate symbol of God's eternal, that is time-giving faithfulness. "Where, O death, is your victory? Where, O death, is your sting?" (1 Cor. 15:55). This is the triumphant note of the Easter hymn with which Christian communities sing praises to their risen Lord.

This resurrection hope is the basis of endurance in the ecodomical covenant. It is a constancy that is loyal to time itself and does not allow even the closeness of death to deprive us of the assurance that our time is open and that each moment is full of blessing.

God's covenantal faithfulness is the life-force of our ecodomical endurance, and God's covenantal ordinances are the basis of the forms of ecodomical order that we are trying to secure. It is this faithful God to whom we are accountable for our steadfastness. It is this eschatological and forensic horizon that enables our loyalty to rise above all those objections that relate to success. Our commitment to the ecodomical covenant cannot and does not depend on whether we "win the game" or not.

If Christian groups or communities stop first to ask themselves whether their solidarity with the impoverished, their struggle against militarism or any other commitment is really going to be successful, they should not even begin any such action, for then their efforts will dwindle to nothing and vanish like straw before fire.

"Does it pay?" This question leads astray. No martyr asks, "What's in it for me?" No one who has truly loved has ever asked, "What do I get out of it?". Of course the ideology of the competitive society proclaims that we should only do what "counts". This opportunistic profit-oriented thought and behaviour is essentially cynical because it instrumentalizes our most important energies.

Work in ecodomical covenant demands endurance, persistence and an intrepid kind of patience: not the stoicism of Sisyphus or the heroism of Prometheus, but the loving faithfulness, prepared for suffering, that Jesus lived. This is the endurance that is rooted in the power of the *pneuma*.

If we trust in this Spirit, then basically we have no other choice than to be loyal and unremittingly faithful. If we are unfaithful we betray the fire of the Spirit within us and thus the essential summons of our own humanity.

There is no need to repeat what we said about endurance in chapter 16. It is essential here only to underscore that the eco-domical covenant lives by intercession, which spreads a fine network of loving commemoration over the whole earth. In this we remember those who have already left us, consider those who otherwise are forgotten and think of those who will come after us.

Endurance proves its power of resistance precisely in situations of persecution, antagonism and suffering. It relies on the power of consoling community and reveals it in the midst of those who are about to despair.

Faithful people are stewards of time. But faithfulness must also pause occasionally to catch its breath. There is no end to endurance, though there are various focal points for forms of commitment that need our reliable service in order to succeed. Our commitment can also be redirected; it has to be open to receive a new emphasis as new needs arise. In the ecodomical covenant we have to make ourselves available and open to changing options and necessities. Partnerships between churches can be dissolved in order to make room for new ones. Endurance in the covenant does not mean that we are indissolubly chained to one another, but that we support and advance one another reciprocally, always trusting in the power of the Spirit, who strengthens us in our weakness.

NOTE

[1] *The Human Condition*, p.244.

Chapter 22

Imagining the Peace of Creation: Suggestions for an Ecodomical Agenda

It is sometimes said that the theologies of the Middle Ages were theologies of love and those of the Reformation were theologies of faith. Is there a term to characterize theologies of the post-modern period? My suggestion is that the guiding concept must be the "peace of creation", or, to use Thomas Berry's term, *pax Gaia*,[1] the peace of the earth.

Many would argue that peace is far too "pretty" a concept to describe adequately the harsh combative structures at work on earth. They regard the evolutionary struggles of the universe and on this planet in terms of warfare. On this view, peace is an idyllic pause between battles or, at the end of it all, the peace of the graveyard. But the peace of creation to which I am referring is not the proverbial calm after the storm but the sustaining power at the heart of all storms.

The anthropologist A.L. Kroeber has noted that "the ideal situation for any individual or any culture is not exactly 'bovine placidity'". Rather, it is "the highest state of tension that the organism can bear creatively".[2] This view suggests that peace is a process in which all life-forms can unfold their energies as creatively as possible and necessary for survival. The term "tension" indicates that conflicts and antagonism cannot be avoided, but must be resolved in a manner which enhances creativity. Nor does peace depend on affluence; in fact, it must be able to make the best use of scarce resources. In such ways Mother Earth has managed to sustain situations of extreme tension by providing increasingly complex "solutions".[3] Peace breaks down when tension exceeds the level at which it can be sustained creatively. In other words, wars reflect the breakdown of creative processes, violent "short-cuts" that destroy rather than build up life-enhancing options. Violence itself may be described as a lack of imagination; it reduces the possibilities of mind and heart to the brute force of the fist and the gun.

For the Greek philosopher Heraclitus, war was "the father of all things" — a classic example of the "patriarchal ego" which has caused so much devastation.[4] For life on earth, peace is the mother of all things. Only if we recognize that creative tensions are the hallmark of peace can we begin to appreciate the polarities our planet has learned to accommodate. It works in a precisely balanced "functional integrity"[5] that can ward off even violent ruptures and dislocations. If we understand this functional integrity as the peace of creation, we have to take into account not merely growth and maturity but also suffering and collapse.[6]

We are living at a dramatic moment in the history of this planet. In an unprecedented manner, the peace of the entire biosphere has become dependent on human decision. In a very short period of time — a mere twinkling of an eye in the history of the planet — the human being, one of myriad species which had been harmless to the earth for millions of years, has acquired the power to endanger the well-being of all life and to upset its functional integrity. In other words, humans are at war with the earth. It has become a total war and, like all total wars, it turns out to be totally suicidal.

More and more people are realizing that this is the crisis which needs to be faced. The war with earth itself must end. That is the epochal challenge before us. The Tower of Babel, that powerful image of patriarchal domestication and dominion, must give way to "greenhouses", that is to matriarchal images of habitation and nurturing. The way we look at ourselves and our role in the world needs to undergo a profound reorientation. We humans dare no longer see ourselves as lordly masters of the earth or as strangers whose true home is elsewhere; we must recognize that we are members of the earth community whose well-being depends wholly on the well-being of the planet.

So the epochal project of our time is indeed an ecodomical one. It has to do with hopeful and constructive work for cultures of habitation. The solution is not a romantic "return to nature". Wherever human beings settle they transform nature into culture. The challenge before us is to create cultures which are compatible with the ways nature works or are at least safely within the carrying capacities of the various ecosystems.

The magnitude of the task before this generation is stupendous. No wonder that numbing is a global epidemic. It takes the combined energies of truth, solidarity and endurance to move out of the enclosures of the numbed soul into the open spaces of creative, purposeful imagination.

The "greenhouse cultures" which need to be built suggest various images which in turn must draw on the collective wisdom of peoples that have learned to adjust to the ecosystems in which they flourish. It would be totally wrong to aim at one single global blueprint for sustainable development. But it is possible to identify a few major points which need to be worked out if the war with the earth is to come to an end.

What would be the central items of such a peace treaty that might usher in the new age whose name has not yet appeared? In this chapter I shall outline some vital points that need to be addressed by religious communities committed to ecodomical renewal. Needless to say, there is not space to deal with them extensively in the context of this book.

Protecting the cosmic goods

"The best things in life are free," according to popular wisdom. What are the best things? Those which are of existential urgency: clean air to breathe, pure water to drink, land on which to dwell in safety, time to live meaningfully, experiences to share creatively. These are the cosmic goods, the "global commons",[7] and they must be free and accessible to every living organism. That is to say, they cannot and should not be owned, sold or bought.

1. Clean air to breathe. Until recently, it was taken for granted that the air above our heads is inexhaustible and eternal. Households and industries used to discharge their poisonous gases freely into the air. It is a recent discovery that the mantle of air which surrounds our planet is slowly being destroyed, its ozone layer dissolving. These examples demonstrate that ecodomical imagination is required to maintain air as a cosmic good.

2. Pure water to drink. If humanity does not soon learn fairly and equitably to administer the earth's water reserves, bitter wars will break out over access to and control of this vital good. Pure water sustains our lives. It is the most important element of health care. The reprocessing of used and polluted water from sewage systems and industrial plants constitutes a tremendous task in most parts of the world. To restore rivers, lakes and oceans to their functional integrity and fertile abundance requires great imaginative efforts, technical skills and international co-operation.

3. A safe place. Every living species needs a place in which it can dwell safely. To destroy this place is as disastrous as to deny it air and water. So every human being needs a place to live, a proper space in which he or she can move about, put down roots, propagate and die. This is why land used to be regarded as something holy, for not only did it provide our home, but in a more existential sense we were seen as part of that home — "dust from dust, earth from earth", as the ancient formula says.[8] As the world population grows, so grows the hunger for land. Because the sharpest mark of poverty is landlessness, "land-reform", that is the development and administration of just schemes for the distribution of land, has become one of the most urgent political tasks today.

4. *Time to fulfil the circle of life.* The fact that each living organism needs its proper time is often overlooked. The relationships among living organisms are interactions that take place on various time-scales and at different rhythms. Everything that lives needs its own genuine time for birthing, growing, maturing and dying. The time that a species requires cannot be regulated, of course, but the right to life implies the possibility of living life in all its fullness — which is why we react with visceral horror to the death of a child. A good life not only requires a safe place, but also needs time to settle and take root. The extension of history back into the past and ahead to the future is an essential component of being at home.

5. *Free sharing of information.* Every living organism, at all levels of organic life, is there to share. It has information on hand. The more complex the organism, the greater its need to receive and to share information. The consciousness of human beings thus depends directly on their capacity to exchange information of all kinds, ranging from genetic information to technical skills to scientific research to the production of Mozart's *Requiem*. The wealth of knowledge, cultural techniques and wisdom accumulated over the ages is a cosmic good.

To say that air, water, land, time and knowledge are cosmic goods has staggering consequences for ethics, economics and politics. Jeremy Rifkin has argued that the gravest problem which has set humankind on its ecocidal course is the "enclosing of the global commons"[9] which began in Europe five hundred years ago. First the commons of villages were enclosed by the landlords; later, large corporations secured for themselves the use of resources in the earth or under the seas. In our time, extensive areas of scientific research are being bought and owned by private organizations. Large firms own communication channels by which information is shared, withheld or manipulated. Efforts are underway to decipher the genetic code of human beings in order to ensure large profits to private institutions.

These processes of privatization are not just the outcome of an excessive need for security, as Rifkin suggests. They are also closely connected with property rights. The idea that cosmic goods can be transferred into private property by way of *occupatio* dates back to Roman times and became the leading legal concept at the end of the Middle Ages.[10] In ancient Rome all things thought to belong to nobody (and thus called *res nullius*, a category which included land, water, animals and plants but also human beings, especially women) could legally be "occupied". Since these things did not possess any religious or philosophical value or standing on their own, occupation was ultimately a question of power. Property rights were seen in absolute terms, subject to no limits in time or in kind. This included unlimited possession, the right to use or abuse property without interference from other parties and the obligation of the state to protect private property.

Clearly this concept of private property is the fundamental motif underlying today's reckless privatization of cosmic goods. When we say that these cosmic goods must be protected and the global commons reopened, we must also begin the discussion about how private property rights can be transformed. This is a task as formidable as the abolition of slavery. The problems to be faced are enormous. In order to find sustainable and just solutions we shall have to consult the wisdom of traditional societies (including the legal concepts of mediaeval Europe). If air, water, land, time and knowledge are cosmic properties, humans can only *enjoy* their use, not own them — which calls for the rediscovery and elaboration of leasing and tenancy rights. Since human beings need their share of the cosmic goods in order to live, humanity might be regarded as an international and intergenerational community of shareholders. And ways will have to be established to set limits to the use and abuse of the world, dependent on ecosystemic conditions and population pressures.

This argument is of special relevance to the issue of intellectual property rights. The knowledge and wisdom of humanity as it has been accumulated over the centuries and is being generated day by day must be regarded as belonging to a cosmic library open to use by all. The wealth of scientific research, artistic expression and cultural technique must remain universally accessible. When private corporations own substantial parts of scientific and technological knowledge, the public loses not only access to them but also the possibility of controlling their rightful use.

Preparing for the post-petroleum age

The source of the physical energies that propelled the advance of modern industrialized societies was at first coal and then, in the 20th century, petroleum and related fossil fuels. It is now estimated that the earth's reserves of oil will be largely depleted around 2030. Humanity has to prepare itself for the post-petroleum-age. [11]

Again, this is a staggering challenge. The implications for industrial production, transportation and heating can hardly be overestimated. But in order to avoid large-scale collapses, which would invariably produce serious conflicts, we need to surmount our denial mechanisms and envisage an age that will thrive on solar, wind, water, biomass and thermal energies. The energies are there; what is needed is the imagination to rearrange our priorities and actually to see the new options. What will have to be the contours of the post-petroleum age?

1. Regional markets. Without oil, international mass transportation will decrease drastically. This must entail a dramatic growth of regional markets. The global system, which depends on the production and shipment of raw materials, will be weakened in order to make room for regionalized and diversified production. This argument has been presented most forcefully by economist Herman Daly and theologian John B. Cobb Jr. They are convinced that the present world economic system has to give way to another that develops within and on the basis of local and regional areas and satisfies the needs of local communities as well as the rhythms of nature and the rights of coming generations. [12]

This process of "redirecting" will also apply to mass tourism. International travelling will be different, probably less rapid and hectic, and at a slower and more intensive pace. Much of international communication will rely on data-based computer systems.

2. Rediscovery of cultural variety. With the increase of regional markets and diversified production techniques, it will become important to listen closely to traditional ways of agricultural and industrial production and to transform them to meet new needs. The variety of cultures is a great asset in designing ways of life that are both humanly dignified and ecologically compatible. This poses exciting opportunities for architecture, systems of health care and the clothing industry, to cite only three examples.

3. *The "greening" of the cities.* "By the end of the twentieth century half of humanity will be urban," states the "Caring for the Earth" survival strategy.[13] By the year 2000 there will be more than 200 large cities, some with more than 20 million inhabitants. These mega-cities will pose extreme challenges to regional markets and support structures. It will not suffice to stop their growth; it will be mandatory to transform them in such ways as to render them tolerable both for human beings and their supportive ecosystem. Curitiba and Singapore are two examples of what can be done if political will and creative imagination join hands. The "greening" of the cities consists in more than planting trees. It entails fighting violence, starvation and ignorance, especially in slums and squatter areas. For example, home gardening, not just in rural but also in urban settings, could considerably relieve economic straits and also contribute to healing the "madness" of the cities.[14]

4. *Disarming the nations.* One of the most powerful elements of the centralized global economy and geopolitics is the military-industrial complex. The arms trade is no doubt the most important factor contributing to the violence between nations and ethnic groups. It also squanders fossil fuel resources and burdens the carrying capacity of the earth. Jeremy Rifkin rightly underlines that "biospheric cultures" — what we have tried to envisage with the image of the "greenhouse culture" — "will require a significant demilitarization of the planet".[15]

New images of respectable poverty

The carrying strength of the earth would obviously collapse if every human being were to enjoy the consumption standards of the average person in the USA or Europe. On the other hand, to continue the contemporary patterns of distribution between the abject misery of the majority of human beings and the equally abject affluence of the minority will equally result in cataclysmic convulsions that the earth cannot bear. Ecodomical imagination is required to find ways out of this impasse.

Given the human condition, we cannot expect to design social systems that would level off all differences between human beings. This was a fallacy of the centralized socialist states and, indeed, one of their most despicable features. There is no single blueprint for social justice, but it is possible — and indeed necessary — to adjust and correct the inordinate injustices of the present world situation. What is needed are some images of what might be called respectable poverty, and the ways to get there must be different.

1. From sub-human misery to respectable poverty. It is said that out of Mexico City's twenty million inhabitants, five million live without even the most primitive sanitary systems. This is but one of many examples that could be cited to describe what I mean by sub-human misery. For this there is no justification. People who live in situations of extreme wretchedness and squalor must be enabled to move into situations which meet their basic needs, among which are the cosmic goods already mentioned, but also the possibility to work for a decent wage, access to health care, housing, schooling and professional training, a fair share in political decision-making and — last but not least — some time for recreation, rituals and festivals. The "option for the poor", the battle-cry of liberation theologies around the world, must be understood as an option against misery and a search for systems of social security that break the vicious circles of despair and chaos.

2. From inhuman affluence to frugal living. It is well known that the wealth of the earth is being concentrated among an increasingly smaller portion of the human race. Excessive consumption and waste by a fraction of the world's people create an inordinate burden for the human community and the ecosystems. Although enormous amounts of money are still spent on making people feel good about this wastefulness, more and more are beginning to realize that the concentration on buying and selling impairs the dignity of human beings, their self-esteem and sense of purpose in life. Consumerism has become the opiate of the masses, with alcoholism, smoking and drugs being particularly dangerous forms of this addiction. So ways are being sought to move towards frugal life-styles, to *have* fewer things in order to *be* a saner person. For rich people the "option for the poor" is a liberation from the addiction to material goods and false securities in order to discover the gratifying power of being and sharing.

3. *Population control.* Images of respectable poverty and frugality need to be supplemented by unequivocal decisions for controlling the population growth on earth. Economic and cultural reasons play a sombre role in this problem, which continues to be highly controversial among religious people. Rosemary Radford Ruether puts it succinctly: "Humanity has no real alternative to population control. The question is, do we want population control to happen voluntarily, before conception, or violently by war, famine, and disease?"[16] She is also correct in affirming that "the empowerment of women as moral agents of their own sexuality and reproduction is... an integral part of any authentic population policy".[17] Although it is important to insist on the responsibility of men for their sexual behaviour, it is essential to free women from their traditional dependencies and to enable them to take an active role in the planning of families.

4. *The matriarchal shift.* The search for "greenhouse cultures" depends in a very decisive way on the role the women of the world are able and allowed to play. Building cultures of habitation and nurturing presupposes what we might call a matriarchal shift in human consciousness. This means not only that women need to play a greater part in elaborating new models and programmes at every level of society, including the global, but also that men must be prepared to change their accustomed roles and behavioural patterns to allow their own female and maternal elements to surface more clearly. Caring, sharing and nurturing are motherly qualities, but not biologically reserved to women. In other words, the "matriarchal shift" that is needed should not be construed as a new war between the sexes but as an option that transforms both male and female stereotypes.

5. *Strengthening the civil society.* Transformations such as these are so vast, conflictive and urgent that governments or international agencies may be tempted to resort to dictatorial measures. We are already experiencing far-reaching breakdowns of national governments. Warring clans and criminal gangs are contributing to the "ungovernability" of many states. On the other hand, people get tired of worrying all the time. They call for "clear-cut" decisions, not wishing forever to be confronted with complex issues. Therefore, special attention must be given to groups and agencies committed to strengthening the participatory structures of democratic decision-making. Though the tasks and functions of such groups vary greatly from one part of the world

to another, they can be described as belonging to the "civil society", a term that denotes citizens' activities located between the purely private and the governmental or military sectors of society.

The changes that confront this generation call for new communal agents, since the traditional carriers of public policy — political parties, commerce, the armed forces, government — appear to be too much tied to the traditional options. The peace of the earth calls for women and men who are bold enough to leave accustomed patterns of thought and pave the way for a future worth living. It is devoutly to be hoped that the religions of the world will learn to move beyond their traditional positions, aware of the beliefs they hold in common, namely that all life is sacred and that we are sisters and brothers, regardless of colour, race, class or nation, since we are all children of God.[18]

* * *

Again, the list of concerns and needs sketched out here in very rough strokes is not intended as representative, much less complete. The notes to this chapter refer to strategies that are much more exhaustive and comprehensive.[19] My purpose has simply been to indicate that there is a direct line between a theology of the Spirit and an ethic for the earth. The energy that keeps creation on its course also manifests itself in the imaginative energies of women and men. Humility, boldness and generosity of spirit are required to keep on envisioning a good life in the face of so much anxiety and violence. The Spirit of life that comes into its own in conscious, believing, loving minds is the heart and soul of ecodomical renewal.

NOTES

[1] Thomas Berry, *The Dream of the Earth*, San Francisco, 1988, p.220.
[2] Quoted by Berry, *ibid.*, p.219.
[3] Cf. B. Swimme and T. Berry, *The Universe Story: From the Primordial Flaring Forth to the Ecozoic Era — A Celebration of the Unfolding of the Cosmos*, San Francisco, 1992.
[4] Cf. Theodore Roszak, *The Voice of the Earth*, New York, 1992, p.215 — although Roszak does not refer his critique of patriarchalism to ancient authors but to contemporary "warrior" imagery, especially in the media (pp.242f.).

[5] Berry, *op. cit.*, p.218.

[6] Cf. J.B. McDaniel, *Of God and Pelicans: A Theology of Reverence for Life*, Louisville, 1989, esp. pp.19ff.

[7] Cf. Jeremy Rifkin, *Biosphere Politics: A Cultural Odyssey from the Middle Ages to the New Age*, San Francisco, 1991, esp. pp.309ff.

[8] This point is presented convincingly in Shannon Jung, *We are Home: A Spirituality of the Environment*, New York, 1993.

[9] Rifkin, *op. cit.*, esp. pp.38ff.

[10] Cf. M. Brocker, *Arbeit und Eigentum: Der Paradigmenwechsel in der neuzeitlichen Eigentumstheorie*, Darmstadt, 1992, pp.30ff; K. Bosselmann, *Im Namen der Natur: Der Weg zum ökologischen Rechtsstaat*, Darmstadt, 1992, pp.98f.

[11] Cf. Rosemary Radford Ruether, *Gaia and God: An Ecofeminist Theology of Earth Healing*, San Francisco, 1992, pp.259ff.

[12] Cf. *For the Common Good: Redirecting the Economy towards Community, the Environment and a Sustainable Future*, Boston, 1989.

[13] Published by Mitchell Beazley in association with IUCN (the World Conservation Union), UNEP (United Nations Environment Programme) and WWF (World Wide Fund for Nature), London, 1993, p.78.

[14] Cf. Roszak, *op. cit.*, p.218.

[15] *Op. cit.*, p.300.

[16] *Op. cit.*, p.263.

[17] *Ibid.*, p.264.

[18] An excellent statement of this is the Declaration of the Parliament of World Religions, Chicago, 1993.

[19] I would especially recommend the "Caring for the Earth" report (note 13 above), although it does not address the essential issue of private property rights.

Chapter 23

Celebrations of Peace

Working for the peace of creation is not the only way in which ecodomical communities must bear witness to the sacramental dignity of life. It is vitally important to understand and appreciate that life is there to be celebrated.

The sacrament of the Sabbath

Jürgen Moltmann reminds us that the world is hallowed as creation primarily through the Sabbath.[1] The Priestly account of creation does not end with the appearance on earth of human beings but climaxes in the institution of the seventh day as God's own day of rest (Gen. 2:2-3).

The biblical myth tells us that God had to rest on the seventh day because the labour of creation had demanded all God's strength. Creation is an outpouring of God, a birthing process, from which God has to recover on the seventh day. The myth insists that the day of rest belongs to the six working days and that without it the process of creation would be out of balance. If there were no day of rest, the work on creation would have to continue in a feverish expansion. But with the Sabbath it is not only God who takes a rest. All of creation has time to recover, too, and thus to discover its proper rhythm. The day of rest is a way of being at peace.

Mythical accounts convey primordial structures of being and reveal fundamental ordinances of life. So when the myth tells us what is good and blessed in God, it also shows us what is good and full of blessing for God's creatures. When God rests on the seventh day, the creation is complete: an appropriate rhythm of life and work has been established for the future. Thus the commandment says: "Remember the sabbath day, and keep it holy. Six days you shall labour and do all your work. But the seventh day is a sabbath to the Lord your God; you shall not do any work — you, your son or your daughter, your male or female slave, your livestock or the alien resident in your towns" (Ex.

20:8-10). This is a way of establishing the ordinance of time in God's sense. The Bible does not see time as so ordered that one day follows the other in eternal similarity, but represents it as being in accord with a rhythmic law. After six working days comes the day of rest, which gives us a weekly rhythm. After six working years comes a sabbatical year, a year of rest for human beings, animals and the earth itself, which gives us the sabbatical rhythm of human life. After seven times seven rhythmic sequences of years comes the year of jubilee, when the social conditions of the people of God are re-established in accordance with the original ordinances (cf. Lev. 25).

This biblical ratio of six to one is neither merely cyclical nor simply linear. The process it describes is one of moving onwards and pausing, of purposeful labour and peaceful contemplation. The notion of continual, indeed unstoppable, progress, which has acquired a quasi-religious significance in modern times, cannot be reconciled with this scriptural understanding of time.

The rhythm of working days and Sabbath also implies a process of use and recreation which is especially significant for dependent people (serfs, women servants, foreign slaves) and for beasts of burden and agricultural plants. This rhythm ensures that people are not exhausted by their labour, but regularly distance themselves from it, which is therapeutically important. In allowing for regular periods of recreation for foreign workers and slaves as well as for nature, this conception of time also protects their dignity as creatures. Finally, by setting limits to the exploitation of humankind and nature, it guarantees justice. And it is through this kind of justice that the peace of creation is maintained.

When the Sabbath is not respected, the other six working days also lose their blessing. If we ignore this rhythm we harm not only ourselves but also all other parts of creation.

Although this conception of time was established in an agrarian era and is associated with farming practices, it is not dependent on peasant conditions of long ago. Down into our own age, believing Jews have observed the Sabbath with impressive determination and under the most varied cultural and social conditions. The Sabbath would not have survived if it were no more than an ancient agrarian custom. Rather, it is an example of primordial wisdom. Strict observance of the Sabbath is more than an act of obedience to God; it offers those who experience it a special curative blessing, for it enriches and supports the life of individuals as well as that of their families, their communities and the entire people. In this respect the Sabbath is like a sacrament which allows God's beneficent presence to shine forth, so that life is endowed and sanctified with special meaning. Hence the Sabbath is both the remembrance of the goodness of creation and the anticipation of the final day of redemption. Stretched between remembrance and anticipation, the Sabbath obtains its messianic dignity, giving sacramental beauty to prayer, rest and love.

The Christian churches have nothing comparable to this. Early on, Christian practice became estranged from observance of the Sabbath because the celebration of the resurrection of the crucified Jesus "on the first day of the week" took centre stage. When the Christian faith was made the official religion of the Roman Empire the "day of the sun" was associated with this Christian observance, but "Sunday" never became what the Sabbath was and is for Judaism.

Can we leave it at that? Must we concede that the observance of a holy day cannot be maintained under the conditions of contemporary industrialized life?

As Christian communities, we are minorities in our various countries (even when we are officially in the majority). We can claim from our societies only what we are personally and as communities ready to profess and practise. Our conduct and devotion must testify to what we regard as important. As minorities we have to bear special witness to the other path — the alternative to the "way of the world". As in the time of Paul, the community of Jesus Christ today is a "nonconformist" movement in which neither routine nor custom predominates but the quest is constantly pursued, through thought and action, for "what is holy and acceptable to God" (Rom. 12:2). Observance of the Sabbath ordinances is an eminently appropriate way to continue that quest.

Moltmann suggests that Christians should adopt the practice of making Saturday afternoon and evening and Sunday morning a special time of celebration: a Sabbath-Sunday feast-day.[2] This should be a quite explicit time of rest, during which the working burden of ordinary weekdays is set down, the household tasks usually relegated to the weekend put aside, and the automobile, television and other machines left idle. The Sabbath-Sunday break should become an ecological time of rest, so that nature too has an opportunity to celebrate its own Sabbath.

This proposal is important not only for over-stressed people in the industrialized nations but also for those in the third world, where the pain of unrelenting struggle deprives people of any chance to distance themselves from their misery, and they run the risk of becoming psychological and spiritual victims of their wretched impoverishment. Salvadorean theologian Jon Sobrino, who happened to be abroad when six of his Jesuit brothers, the housekeeper and her daughter were murdered, admits that the workload of his community had become so heavy that they no longer rested on Sundays. The very notion of holidays, much less a sabbatical leave, disappeared completely from their thoughts.[3] This may sound heroic, and it was probably inevitable under the circumstances of repression in El Salvador, but it is in itself an expression of misery. We dare not set aside the rhythms of work and rest in the long run. This is no luxury of wealthy societies but a piece of great wisdom, revealed in ancient times for the well-being of all creatures. Eventually a human being without rest turns into an agitated Titan or the slave of a technological and industrial economy that recognizes only unceasing "progress" but has nothing in common with the real "economy" of living things.

As I have suggested earlier, Christian communities should seek to establish a worldwide network of ecodomical centres. A universal community of this kind is necessary to give the Sabbath-Sunday new meaning as a time of rest. There is no other way to offer the mutual help needed to learn the discipline appropriate to this sacrament of creation-peace and to provide spaces where the overburdened can find true care and protection.

It is clear that the biblical Sabbath ordinances have social and ecological consequences. The silencing of automobile engines on "car-free Sundays", for example, would have a major significance, not least symbolically, for the motor vehicle is one of the most powerful idols of industrial society. Even more influential, as far as the social structure of our societies is concerned, would be the introduction of sabbatical years for all working people, not just for a few academics. The regular interruption of one's work by a sabbatical year after every six working years would make much more sense than the arrangement now prevalent: the threefold division of life into school education and professional training, active working life and retirement (a division which ignores that a very considerable section of the population is unemployed). The "reinvention of work"[4] implies a reinvention of rest and celebration.

Such life-renewing rhythms of work and rest are also urgently needed in agriculture. We pay a heavy price for using chemical fertilizers to ensure permanent fertility, for this is possible only at the cost of irreparable ecological damage. Restoring the Sabbath ordinances would aim at a creative and lasting communion of nature and humankind.

We need the Sabbath-Sunday rhythms to rediscover the space for the holy rituals which help us to understand the sacramental structure of creation and the blessings it can afford. We need these holy times to regain the appropriate discipline, so that God's life-promoting blessing can become manifest among us.

When we recognize the Sabbath-Sunday as the original sacrament of God's sanctifying grace, we can see how the two central sacraments of Christianity, baptism and the eucharist, grew from this soil. These two sacraments are the covenantal feasts of universal Christendom.

Baptism: by water and the Spirit

From the start, Christian baptism was more than the initiation rite of a new sect. It was the symbol of incorporation into the "body of Christ", of citizenship of the kingdom of God. Even more fundamentally, it symbolized entry into life in the new creation. In baptism, Christ's death and resurrection were symbolically repeated in immersion and re-emergence, discarding the old vesture and putting on a new robe. Baptism is not a rite of cleansing which needs to be repeated regularly, nor is it an act of marking the human body, or parts of it, as is the case in various rites of circumcision. Baptism is the sacrament of rebirth. It is a unique, unrepeatable process with universally human and even cosmic implications. Ultimately, only one thing corresponds to baptism: creation itself.

Water and Spirit are the original elements of life. The history of creation starts with them. According to Genesis 1:2, the *rûah* makes water creative, and without water *rûah* remains as fleeting as the wind. The ecological crisis has taught us anew that the matrix of all sentient life is pure water and pure air. When water and air are polluted, death can enter into us through every pore.

There is thus no more fundamental way to express incorporation into the community of Christ. But this rebirth and new

creation does not imply any devaluation of the first creation —
a misunderstanding as old as the sacrament itself. Paul maintains that baptism is not a new creation in the sense that it
diminishes the worth of the old one. Against this gnostic error,
he stresses that in baptism the Spirit of Christ has received
power over us — the Spirit who from the beginning was in God
and who built the house of creation. In the resurrection of the
crucified one, this power reveals its force: the energy of love,
ready to incur every kind of sacrifice and not to be conquered
by any kind of death. In the communities of the risen Christ,
this energy is seeking to be born, striving to see the light of
day.

As the sacrament of a rebirth in which God's *rûah* brings us
illumination and, in the light of Easter morning, enables us to
recognize the world and our place in it, baptism becomes the
sacrament of empowerment. It allows us to lead our lives in the
light of truth, solidarity and endurance. Life in the power of the
Holy Spirit is a life of sanctification and holiness.

In pietistic and fundamentalist churches, a "holy life" has
often been associated with individual moral integrity. "Live by
the Spirit, and do not gratify the desires of the flesh" (Gal. 5:16)
— this and similar precepts from the epistles of the New Testament have served as iron yard-sticks for God-fearing people. I do
not I mean to discredit efforts by Christian men and women to
lead a responsible life. As a matter of fact, all the baptized are
reminded by their baptism of the sanctity of their body and the
dignity of their creatureliness. They are summoned to demonstrate this dignity and holiness in their way of life and through
service to others.

This propriety and discipline are among the effects of the
pneuma. Often, however, discipline is practised out of fear. The
result is a mixture of anxiety and restrictiveness that has nothing
to do with dedication and generosity. Paul wrote to Timothy:
"God did not give us a spirit of cowardice, but rather a spirit of
power and of love and self-discipline" (2 Tim. 1:7). In other
words, the discipline that emanates from the *pneuma* has to do
with strength and love. It does not thrive at the expense of others,
but seeks their welfare in all things. Such sanctification does not
despise the world and the miracles of our body, but develops in
the dimension of celebration, where joy at the marvels of creation
is united with glorification of the Creator. Sanctification in this

sense is also a resistance movement against all forces that want to destroy this blessing God has bestowed on his creation.

Important as this personal dimension of baptism is, we must not forget that it also has a cosmic frame of reference. The water of baptism is fresh, flowing water. If pure water is part of the holiness of the sacrament, then keeping water pure is part of the practice of holiness. Thus baptism has a cosmic and ecodomical relevance. As Thomas Berry remarks: "If the water is polluted, it can neither be drunk nor used for baptism. Both in its physical reality and in its psychic symbolism, it is a source not of life, but of death."[5]

The intimate association between baptismal water and drinking water is also part of its sacramental quality. Baptismal water already possesses some part of the power of the divine word pronounced over it, for it is the original element of life.

The practice of sanctification must also correspond to these cosmic implications of baptism. Holiness of life also has to do with the healing of the world, with the purification of the water in springs, rivers, lakes and oceans. Anyone who baptizes children but apathetically allows this future generation to be cheated by the reckless pollution of water is betraying both the sacrament and the children.

It would be appropriate to develop a new rite that would highlight the reality that baptism has its existential locus in the sanctification of creation. I would suggest something like an annual baptismal commemoration in the springtime, the season of planting, with clear symbolic and ecological connotations. (In the northern hemisphere, these links could be further underlined by scheduling the commemoration between Easter and Pentecost.) Baptismal commemoration could be associated with a festival of planting trees, one for each individual baptized in the preceding year. This could be done on church land or at a suitable spot in the community, and would be cared for by parents and by the children themselves over the years. If the community understood the intimate relationship between baptism and planting, between blessing and growing, these young trees would be well cared for. In the course of the years "baptismal forests" would grow around many communities. Although such a new rite could not compensate for the devastation of our forests, it might raise awareness and eventually even have political effects.

Finally, we should not overlook another aspect of baptism which has considerable ecodomical implications. Despite great liturgical variety, almost all churches understand baptism as inclusion in the kingdom of Christ. They agree that the "household" into which we are baptized must not be understood in a narrow ecclesiocentric sense but in terms of creation theology. Accordingly, baptism should be seen as the sacrament that initiates the unity of the churches. The church's unity (*koinonia*) is established not through the eucharist, but through baptism.

If baptism is the decisive sign and sacrament of unity, this has considerable implications for the debate about what constitutes the full communion of the churches. This in turn has consequences for the practice of baptism. Its administration should be arranged so that it becomes a much more explicitly central occasion of parish life. The ecodomical nature of baptism should be brought out by ecumenical services on central baptism days, say on Easter morning. If the churches in a town could join in celebrating feasts of baptism, the community-building impact of this sacrament could be clearly manifested. Although it takes place in our local communities, our baptism calls us far beyond, making us members of a household that comprises heaven and earth.

The eucharist: the Sabbath-feast in the ecodomical covenant

The roots of the eucharist are found in the Passover meal, the commemoration of Israel's liberation from slavery in Egypt. More specifically, it celebrates the great preservation on that fateful night when the first-born sons of Egypt were slain (Ex. 12). So the Passover is the feast of preservation in God's covenant.

The gospels tell us that Jesus celebrated the Passover meal with his disciples on the evening before his arrest (Mark 14:12ff. and parallels). This celebration is profoundly marked by a premonition of Jesus' death, which it ritually anticipates. The early Christian community thus made a major change in the significance of the Passover, emphasizing no longer the element of preservation but the sacrifice of God's first-born. Jesus becomes the "Lamb of God who takes away the sin of the world".

It was appropriate to this radical shift of meaning that Christian communities should take as the main sacramental symbols not the lamb, but bread and wine. The bread that is broken signifies the body of Jesus broken on the cross. The wine that is poured out symbolizes the blood that flows from Jesus' wounds.

Bread and wine have their own sacramental qualities. They enable us to see the meaning of the "for you" in Jesus' self-sacrifice. Unfortunately our liturgies do not adequately reflect the brutality with which bread and wine are made. The grain has to be flailed and milled, reduced to flour and baked under great heat. The original power of the wheat, its fertility, is crushed. But with its new function as bread, it is endowed with a new power, for it serves to feed human beings. While the original function of the kernel, to ensure the survival of its species, is destroyed, as bread it serves to guarantee the survival of others. Living for itself is transformed into a life for others. Similarly, the grapes from the vine are crushed and trodden, destroying the fruit but also transforming it, for wine gladdens the human heart (Ps. 104:15). This new function of the wine no longer has anything to do with its former purpose.

Thus it is not only as the product of human labour but also by virtue of the harsh process of their transformation that bread and wine are symbols of that history which comprises the suffering, death and resurrection of Jesus Christ. Bread and wine become signs of a covenant that unites peoples of all nations and races because it relies on the power of Jesus' living for others. This covenantal meal is the sacramental representation of a history of self-emptying and self-sacrifice: a history that accepts death and by that very acceptance leaves death behind. It is also the symbol of a community that is indebted to that total self-surrender and tries to live in such a spirit of self-giving.

When we consume the bread and wine in the power of the *pneuma*, something of that transforming power lives in us, flows through our community and enables it to realize its vocation, which is to serve the peace of creation. So we can conclude: the eucharist is the sacrament-on-the-way for the pilgrim people of God, the celebration of the Sabbath in the ecodomical covenant. We may look briefly at three facets of this.

1. Eucharist and Sabbath. We said earlier in this chapter that the Sabbath has a central significance because it helps us to observe and preserve the rhythm of creation. The blessing of the Sabbath consists in its establishing and maintaining a mode and sense of time that sets a limit to working days and also gives them their due measure, value and thus dignity.

The Sabbath ensures that time is set aside for celebration and for taking distance from work, restlessness and stress. It also opens up a space where we can contemplate "what we have done and what we have left undone" and bring them before God in thanksgiving, confession or, if the burden is very heavy, lamentation and mourning.

This is exactly what happens in the eucharist. It provides the congregation with a space for reflection, contemplation and celebration. It is the place where we learn to give thanks. Thus what we do in everyday life is duly sanctified and also, of course, subjected to critical review.

When we learn to celebrate the eucharist in its true and literal sense as *thanksgiving*, we also learn to glorify God as the ground of our life, something which is generally impossible in the hurly-burly of every day.

If Christian life is seen as life in the ecodomical covenant, that means we not only dedicate ourselves to work for peace, but also thankfully acknowledge this peace as a reality which already surrounds us in various ways without any contribution on our own part. It may often seem that we have nothing to celebrate. But in the calm of the Sabbath and the quiet gathering around the eucharist, we have space and time to discern the marks and signs of grace in insignificant things.

The community of God's pilgrim people can be safeguarded only if there are regular moments of rest along the way. In their eucharistic assemblies the People of God recover from the conflicts and wounds of daily life. So the ecodomical covenant is promoted and extended not only by work but also by means of the regular eucharistic celebrations as highlights of the Christian Sabbath. This is the place where the triad of truth, solidarity and endurance is experienced. In the eucharist we seek and exchange truth, we practise and experience solidarity, and we renew our endurance.

2. *A celebration of charisms.* Although baking bread and making wine involve violent transformations, as we have seen, they keep their original flavour. In everyday life we enjoy the great varieties of bread and wine, their different tastes and characters. We should not lose sight of this when we take bread and wine as elements of the eucharistic celebration, because this tells us something important about the varieties of gifts and energies we bring to the service of Christ, which also have to be transformed in order to reflect the very core of creation, the outpouring of self-sacrificial love.

This implies that we as members of the eucharistic community undergo transformation. Our being for ourselves is changed into being for others. That is our calling. At times it may require great suffering and even martyrdom. Serving the ecodomy of God's kingdom puts our specific gifts and talents in a new horizon. In the fire of our calling they are being corrected, cleansed and refocussed. Our innate abilities are not destroyed but instead appear in a new light. They become gifts of grace, charisms.

This applies not only to individual persons but also to our communities, their forms of devotion, theological traditions and church organizations. These too are energies that can become charisms if they are constantly allowed and enabled to undergo transformation into being for others. It is this being-for-others that keeps the charismatic qualities alive. Without this dimension they lose their ecodomical purpose and become introverted and destructive.

3. *Working for joy.* In the light of all we have said, the eucharist is — or must become — a celebration of unconditional communion. This leads us to consider briefly the much-debated issue of joint eucharistic celebrations of people who belong to divided churches. The perspectives set forth in this book lead to the conclusion that every eucharistic assembly must be essentially accessible to all who seriously wish to participate in it. The sacrament that is the symbol of being-for-others must be essentially available for everyone, and to set up barriers against this is to run counter to the very nature of sacrament.

I have already suggested that it is not the eucharist but the sacrament of baptism which constitutes the unity of the church. Therefore there can be no reason why eucharistic communion should be denied to people who have been bound together in the Spirit through confession and baptism.

To be sure, the frequently used term "eucharistic hospitality" is unfortunate; for the churches are not the lords of the communion table but the invitees to it. Since there is only one Lord of the eucharist, every celebration of it should be an open one. This applies also to celebrations in which all the participants belong to one and the same church. Faith and doubt keep close company in all of them. As to their worthiness, all believers approach the Lord's table in their own particular ways and all stand in need of forgiveness.

Metropolitan Paulos Mar Gregorios of India says that the church re-presents the eucharist, the "sacrament of thanksgiving", in Christ's name and on behalf of the whole of God's creation.[6] But this is possible only for a church wholly conscious of its unworthiness and thus compelled to hope for the grace of God, who alone knows human hearts and is therefore the sole judge of the minds and motives of believers.

Each church lives in the tension between calling and promise. Exposed to the ambiguities of history, it experiences itself as both receptive and closed; as open to God's power yet self-enclosed; as a community of justified sinners and part of the people of God, yet scattered among nations who visit war and violence upon one another.

Metropolitan Gregorios sees the eucharist as the process in which the community represents the entire creation before God. This social dimension is central. But this also means that a church aware of its position between God and creation has to be open and receptive both to God and to creation. Basically, therefore, the church can only understand itself as an open system. In that case, the erection of barriers between one church and others is entirely artificial. How can anyone who denies communion to a neighbour — and a neighbouring church — be an authentic representative of creation? How can a church be faithful in cosmic terms if it fails to be faithful in immediate social contexts?

Metropolitan Gregorios agrees that it is quite possible within the Orthodox tradition to admit non-Orthodox Christians to the eucharist. Canonical authorities can allow this "in cases of urgent pastoral necessity". In the face of such a statement, one is compelled to ask: how can one ignore the deep pain in so many Christian communities, which cries out for common celebration of the eucharist? "Pastoral necessity" may not be understood as a mere "human problem"; it is a genuine setting in which theological knowledge and practice must prove their worth. Therefore, the demand that canonical authorities in the Orthodox and Roman Catholic churches should allow open communion with other Christians and churches acquires new urgency.

Since the need is pressing, fixed dogmatic positions have to change. It is urgent not to obscure any longer the creative relationship between working and celebrating. The task to which all Christians are jointly called requires joint contemplation. This is why the former general secretary of the World Council of Churches, Emilio Castro, exclaimed during the Canberra assembly:

> This should be the last assembly with a divided eucharist! It is not only a passionate *cri du coeur*...; it is also the awareness of our real spiritual danger to prolong an ecumenism without openness to the surprises of the Spirit. Our common pilgrimage will not endure long without the holy anticipation of the kingdom.[7]

This "cry from the heart" of an experienced pastor and veteran ecumenist underscores the urgency with which the question of eucharistic fellowship needs to be treated. For when the churches lose sight of the common eucharist, they are bound also to lose sight of their common way. How are churches to work together if they cannot eat and drink together? Without eucharistic nurture, the pilgrim people of God starve.

To some this may sound like emotional pleading, but in fact it is also coldly realistic. The recurrent denial of eucharistic communion is the root cause of the much-lamented "stagnation" of the ecumenical movement. Precisely when we look on the eucharist as the sacrament of our common way, we maintain its eschatological quality. By strengthening people in the midst of their everyday hardship, it opens up the way into the future. Because we share bread and wine with one another, we learn how to fight for justice between rich and poor. Because we are united at the Lord's table, we become more aware of what separates us and how to overcome it. To regard the common eucharist only as the crowning result once all separations have been overcome seems to me to be misplaced eschatology.

Celebrations of peace are moments when work for the peace of creation regains its promise. The Sabbath-Sunday turns into a blessing of time; baptism is the blessing of our beginnings; and the eucharist is the sacrament which sanctifies the roads we take. These sacraments spare us none of the complexity and difficulty of work in the ecodomical covenant, yet ensure that it proceeds in a setting and expectation of joy. When we celebrate the festivals of peace, we approach the mystery that creation holds in store for us.

God's first and last word is *grace*; our first and last response is *thanksgiving*.

NOTES

[1] Moltmann, *God in Creation*, London, 1985, pp.276-96.
[2] *Ibid.*, p.296.
[3] Sobrino, *Compañeros de Jesus*, Santander, 1989.
[4] The title of Matthew Fox's illuminating book, with the subtitle *A New Vision of Livelihood for Our Time*, San Francisco, 1994.
[5] *The Dream of the Earth*, pp.79f.
[6] Paulos Mar Gregorios, "Not a Question of Hospitality", *The Ecumenical Review*, Vol. 44, 1992, p.46.
[7] Quoted in Kinnamon, *Signs of the Spirit*, p.167.

Bibliography

G. Altner, "The Community of Creation As a Community in Law: The New Contract Between the Generations", in Johann Baptist Metz and E. Schille-beeckx, eds, *No Heaven Without Earth* (*Concilium*, 1991/4), London, SCM Press, 1991.

G. Altner, *Naturvergessenheit: Grundlagen einer umfassenden Bioethik*, Darm-stadt, Wissenschaftliche Buchgesellschaft, 1991.

> Biologist and theologian Günter Altner is one of Germany's leading ecological thinkers. In developing his bio-ethics, he draws on Albert Schweitzer's concept of "life".

H. Arendt, *The Human Condition*, Chicago, Univ. of Chicago Press, 1958.

> This work by the well-known German Jewish philosopher remains a very helpful analysis of the state of consciousness that underlies modern Western life and work.

R. Bellah, R. Madsen, W. Sullivan, A. Swidler, S. Tipton, *Habits of the Heart: Individualism and Commitment in American Life*, New York, Harper & Row, 1985.

> The research of Robert Bellah and his colleagues is important for under-standing the social crisis of contemporary US society and indispensable for a rediscovery of communitarian principles.

T. Berry, *The Dream of the Earth*, San Francisco, Sierra Club Books, 1988.

T. Berry and B. Swimme, *The Universe Story: From the Primordial Flaring Forth to the Ecozoic Era — A Celebration of the Unfolding of the Cosmos*, San Francisco, Harper, 1992.

> The writings of Thomas Berry, grounded in both Christian mystic traditions and scientific expertise, are of prophetic relevance because of the much-needed comprehensive perception of the universe which they provide.

H. Blumenberg, *Die Arbeit am Mythos*, Frankfurt, 1979.

> The German philosophers Hans Blumenberg and Kurt Hübner and the Polish philosopher Leszek Kolakowski develop distinctive approaches to elaborating the relevance for contemporary life of myth and mythic awareness.

L. Boff, *Der Dreieinige Gott*, Düsseldorf, Bibliothek Theologie der Befreiung, 1987.

L. Boff, *Gott kommt früher als Missionar: Neuevangelisierung für eine Kultur des Lebens und der Freiheit*, Düsseldorf, 1991.

L. Boff, *Kleine Trinitätslehre*, Düsseldorf, 1990.

L. Boff, *Saint Francis: A Model for Human Liberation*, London, SCM, 1985.

> A prolific author and one of the founding fathers of Latin American liberation theology, Leonardo Boff incorporates into his political theology not only the radical Franciscan mystic traditions of Europe, but also the ecological heritage of the indigenous peoples in the Americas.

K. Bosselmann, *Im Namen der Natur: Der Weg zum ökologischen Rechtstaat*, Darmstadt, Wissenschaftlicher Buchgesellschaft, 1992.

> Klaus Bosselmann, a German lawyer and philosopher who is now teaching at the University of Auckland, elaborates a framework for international ecological law.

H.E. Daly and John Cobb Jr, *For the Common Good: Redirecting the Economy Toward Community, the Environment and a Sustainable Future*, Boston, Beacon Press, 1989.

> This classic critique of modern economics, co-authored by an economist and a theologian, is indispensable reading for all who recognize the urgent need for a new economic system that links the needs of communities with the requirements of nature and the rights of coming generations.

U. Duchrow, *Europe in the World System 1492-1992: Is Justice Possible?*, Geneva, WCC, 1992.

U. Duchrow, *Global Economy: A Confessional Issue for the Churches?*, Geneva, WCC, 1987.

U. Duchrow and G. Liedke, *Shalom: Biblical Perspectives on Creation, Justice and Peace*, Geneva, WCC, 1989.

> Ulrich Duchrow, German theologian and ecumenical activist, offers trenchant criticisms of the global "neo-liberal" economic system and the destructive impact it has on the third world.

J.R. Engel and J.G. Engel, eds, *Ethics of Environment and Development: Global Challenge, International Response*, Tucson, Arizona, 1990.

> The excellent essays in this collection reflect the international and intercultural search for ecological ethics.

H. Epstein, *Children of the Holocaust*, New York, G.P. Putnam, 1979.

> Helen Epstein's research, based on interviews with children of victims of the Holocaust, helps to understand the intergenerational impact of hurt and the ensuing difficulties of healing.

M. Fox, *The Coming of the Cosmic Christ*, San Francisco, Harper, 1988.

M. Fox, *Original Blessing*, Santa Fe, New Mexico, Bear & Co., repr. 1987.

M. Fox, *The Reinvention of Work: A New Vision of Livelihood for Our Time*, San Francisco, Harper, 1994.

Matthew Fox, a former Catholic who is now an Anglican priest and theologian, has been immensely creative in his search for a new paradigm of creation spirituality that is based on the mystic traditions of humanity.

E. Fromm, *The Anatomy of Human Destructiveness*, New York, Holt, Rinehart & Winston, 1973.

E. Fromm, *To Have or To Be*, London, Jonathan Cape, 1979.

E. Fromm, *Psychoanalyse und Ethik*, Frankfurt, 1981.

The work of the well-known psychologist Erich Fromm has made important contributions to our understanding of the interconnections between the psychic, political and ethical problems in contemporary Western societies.

B. Frost, *The Politics of Peace*, London, Darton, Longman & Todd, 1991.

British lay theologian Brian Frost presents a fascinating picture of how elements of forgiveness are finding their way into politics in all parts of the world.

I. Hedström, *Somos parte de un gran equilibrio: La crisis ecológica en Centroamérica*, 2d ed., San José, 1990.

I. Hedström, *Volverán la golondrinas? La reintegración de la creación desde una perspectiva Latinoamericana*, San José, DEI, 2d ed., 1990.

Hedström, a Swedish biologist and theologian, worked for many years in Latin America. His research is central to understanding the ecological destruction in that region of the globe.

F. Hinkelammert, *La deuda externa de América Latina: El automatismo de la deuda*, San José, DEI, 1988.

Of German origin, Hinkelammert is a Catholic theologian and economist who has spent most of his professional life in Latin America. He is an expert on the debt crisis and its effect on impoverished people.

J.F. Gomez Hinojosa, "De la ecología a la ecofilia: Apuntes para una ecología liberadora", *PASOS*, No. 30, 1990, pp. 7-18.

J.F. Gomez Hinojosa, "Está viva la naturaleza? Apuntes para una ecología liberadora, II", *PASOS*, No. 38, 1991, pp. 1-12.

The Mexican Catholic theologian offers an illuminating perspective on how liberation theology can accommodate ecological concerns.

K. Hübner, *Die Wahrheit des Mythos*, Munich, 1985.

See under Blumenberg above.

S. Jung, *We Are Home: A Spirituality of the Environment*, New York, Paulist, 1993.

> Shannon Jung's book is important for its overcoming of the traditional separation between human beings and nature and for drawing creative consequences from their basic connectedness.

L. Kolakowski, *Die Gegenwärtigkeit des Mythos*, Munich, 1973.

> See under Blumenberg above.

J. Lara, *El Tawantinsuyu: Origen, organización política, económica y social*, Cochabamba and La Paz, Bolivia, 3d ed., 1990.

> Lara, a Bolivian economist and historian, analyzes the social, political and ecological characteristics of the societies in the central Andean region, commonly known as the Inca empire.

R.J. Lifton, *The Broken Connection: On Death and the Continuity of Life*, New York, Basic Books, 1983.

R.J. Lifton, *Death in Life: Survivors of Hiroshima*, New York, 1968.

R.J. Lifton, *The Future of Immortality and Other Essays for a Nuclear Age*, New York, 1987.

R.J. Lifton, *The Life of the Self: Toward a New Psychology*, New York, Touchstone Books, 1976.

R.J. Lifton, *The Nazi Doctors: Medical Killing and the Psychology of Genocide*, New York, Basic Books, 1986.

R.J. Lifton and R. Falk, *Indefensible Weapons: The Political and Psychological Case against Nuclearism*, New York, Basic Books, 1982.

> Lifton's research is central for understanding the psychic disposition of human beings under the massive threats of nuclear and ecological annihilation.

J. McDaniel, *Earth, Sky, Gods and Mortals: Developing an Ecological Spirituality*, Mystic, Connecticut, Twenty-Third Publications, 1990.

J. McDaniel, *Of God and Pelicans: A Theology of Reverence for Life*, Louisville, Westminster/John Knox, 1989.

> Jay B. McDaniel's work offers a "theology of life" that moves beyond traditional anthropocentric concepts of creation. Important for the issue of suffering.

M.D. Meeks, *God the Economist: The Doctrine of God and Political Economy*, Minneapolis, Fortress, 1989.

> M. Douglas Meeks provides a critique of modern economics on the basis of a theology that affirms God as Economist and creation as a single "household".

J. Moltmann, *The Church in the Power of the Spirit: A Contribution to Messianic Ecclesiology*, London, SCM, 1992.

J. Moltmann, *God in Creation: An Ecological Doctrine of Creation*, London, SCM, 1985.

J. Moltmann, *The Spirit of Life: A Universal Affirmation*, London, SCM, 1992.

J. Moltmann, *Theology of Play*, New York, Harper & Row, 1972.

J. Moltmann, *The Trinity and the Kingdom of God*, London, SCM, 1981.

J. Moltmann, *The Way of Jesus Christ: Christology in Messianic Dimensions*, London, SCM, 1990.

> Jürgen Moltmann, German systematic theologian, is internationally renowned for placing his messianic theology in direct contact with global issues.

C. Mulack, *Im Anfang war die Weisheit: Feministische Kritik des männlichen Gottesbildes*, Stuttgart, Kreuz, 1988.

C. Mulack, *Die Weiblichkeit Gottes: Matriarchale Voraussetzungen des Gottesbildes*, Stuttgart, Kreuz, 1983.

> This German feminist theologian emphasizes the matriarchal implications of images of God, especially the sophia-tradition.

W. Pannenberg, *Systematic Theology*, Edinburgh, T. & T. Clark, 1991.

> In his "summa", the well-known German theologian Wolfhart Pannenberg places the problems of classical Christian theology in close context with contemporary issues.

J. Patton, *Is Human Forgiveness Possible?*, Nashville, Abingdon, 1986.

> The Atlanta-based pastoral psychologist emphasizes forgiveness from the point of view of the victims and presents it as a healing process of discovery.

P. Potter, *Life in All Its Fullness*, Geneva, WCC, 1981.

> In this collection of essays the former general secretary of the World Council of Churches and Caribbean theologian places the ecumenical agenda in relation to the biblical meaning of life.

K. Raiser, *Ecumenism in Transition: A Paradigm Shift in the Ecumenical Movement?*, Geneva, WCC, 1991.

> The present general secretary of the World Council of Churches offers his reasons for believing that a necessary "paradigm shift" must take place in the ecumenical movement.

J. Rifkin, *Biosphere Politics: A Cultural Odyssey from the Middle Ages to the New Age*, San Francisco, Harper, 1991.

> In this provocative attempt to arrange the priorities of politics according to the security needs of the biospheric community of life, Rifkin describes the paradigm of modernity as a model of reckless enclosure of the "global commons".

T. Roszak, *The Voice of the Earth*, New York, Simon & Schuster, 1992.

Roszak's immensely informative and persuasive treatise on the need to rethink psychology in terms of the cosmic relatedness of humans with all other life forms calls for a rediscovery of the healing potential of the "voice of the earth".

R.R. Ruether, *Gaia and God: An Ecofeminist Theology of Earth Healing*, San Francisco, Harper, 1992.

The well-known feminist theologian offers not only a critical evaluation of Western Christian culture but at the same time tremendously helpful suggestions as to how the wounds of the earth community can be healed.

P. Teilhard de Chardin, *Das Herz der Materie*, Olten, Walter Verlag, 1990.

The mystical vision of the evolution of cosmic consciousness by the famous French researcher-theologian.

P. Tillich, *Systematic Theology*, Volumes I-III, Chicago, Univ. of Chicago Press, 1957-63.

Remains a classic attempt to relate Christian thought to the issues and problems of contemporary society.

P. Trigo, *Creation and History*, Maryknoll, Orbis, 1991.

Trigo develops a creation theology that is set within the conceptual framework of Latin American liberation theology.

E.U. von Weizsäcker, *Erdpolitik: Ökologische Realpolitik an der Schwelle zum Jahrhundert der Umwelt*, Darmstadt, Wissenschaftliche Buchgesellschaft, 1989.

A highly suggestive attempt to rethink "earth politics" for the requirements of the next century. The German economist and political scientist proposes ecologically sound economic measures which are especially attractive because they are both sustainable and politically feasible.